The Lord provides

RUTH

by Tony Merida

thegoodbook
COMPANY

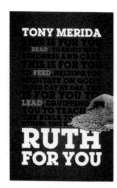

Ruth For You

If you are reading *Ruth For You* alongside this Good Book Guide, here is how the studies in this booklet link to the chapters of *Ruth For You*:

Study One → Ch 1

Study Two → Ch 2-3

Study Three → Ch 4

Study Four → Ch 5

Study Five → Ch 6

Study Six → Ch 7

Study Seven → Ch 8

Find out more about *Ruth For You* at:
www.thegoodbook.com/for-you

The Lord provides

The Good Book Guide to Ruth

© Tony Merida/The Good Book Company, 2020.

Series Consultants: Tim Chester, Tim Thornborough,
Anne Woodcock, Carl Laferton

Published by:
The Good Book Company

thegoodbook.com | thegoodbook.co.uk
thegoodbook.com.au | thegoodbook.co.nz | thegoodbook.co.in

ISBN: 9781784983888 | Printed in Turkey

CONTENTS

Introduction: Good Book Guides

Every Bible-study group is different—yours may take place in a church building, in a home or in a cafe, on a train, over a leisurely mid-morning coffee or squashed into a 30-minute lunch break. Your group may include new Christians, mature Christians, non-Christians, moms and tots, students, businessmen or teens. That's why we've designed these *Good Book Guides* to be flexible for use in many different situations.

Our aim in each session is to uncover the meaning of a passage, and see how it fits into the "big picture" of the Bible. But that can never be the end. We also need to appropriately apply what we have discovered to our lives. Let's take a look at what is included:

⊕ **Talkabout:** Most groups need to "break the ice" at the beginning of a session, and here's the question that will do that. It's designed to get people talking around a subject that will be covered in the course of the Bible study.

⊙ **Investigate:** The Bible text for each session is broken up into manageable chunks, with questions that aim to help you understand what the passage is about. The **Leader's Guide** contains **guidance for questions**, and sometimes ⊻ additional "follow-up" questions.

⊡ **Explore more (optional):** These questions will help you connect what you have learned to other parts of the Bible, so you can begin to fit it all together like a jig-saw; or occasionally look at a part of the passage that's not dealt with in detail in the main study.

⊡ **Apply:** As you go through a Bible study, you'll keep coming across **apply** sections. These are questions to get the group discussing what the Bible teaching means in practice for you and your church. ⊡ **Getting personal** is an opportunity for you to think, plan and pray about the changes that you personally may need to make as a result of what you have learned.

⊡ **Pray:** We want to encourage prayer that is rooted in God's word—in line with his concerns, purposes and promises. So each session ends with an opportunity to review the truths and challenges highlighted by the Bible study, and turn them into prayers of request and thanksgiving.

The **Leader's Guide** and introduction provide historical background information, explanations of the Bible texts for each session, ideas for **optional extra** activities, and guidance on how best to help people uncover the truths of God's word.

Why study Ruth?

The book of *Ruth* is one of the best short stories ever written. We are drawn to the *characters*: grieving Naomi, loyal Ruth, and compassionate Boaz. The *setting* is also intriguing. It takes place during the time of the Judges (Ruth 1:1); and the locations include Bethlehem, Moab, Boaz's field, a threshing floor, a city gate, and a bedroom. The *plot* involves a story of redemption which, as we learn, is part of the grand story of redemption (4:17-22). Naomi stands in the middle of the *conflict* of the book, as a widow with no son to carry on the family's line. At the heart of the *resolution* is Boaz, a figure who shows a lot of similarities to David's greatest son, Jesus.

As well as the fact that it's a beautifully written love story, there are many reasons to study *Ruth*.

First, *we need to see the larger story of God's redeeming grace.* The book of *Ruth* advances the story of God's redeeming grace to Adam's fallen race. It magnifies God's *hesed*—his covenantal faithfulness and unceasing kindness.

Second, *we need a greater appreciation of God's providence.* God is present in the lives of these seemingly insignificant characters, displaying his meticulous providence, just as he is at work in our own lives.

Third, *we need to remember God's global mercy.* The gospel is not for the Jew only, but for the whole world, including Moabites like Ruth.

Fourth, *we need models of genuine godliness.* Ruth inspires us to be loyal, sincere, gracious, courageous, and devoted. Boaz gives us a model of manhood: justice-pursuing and not passive, compassionate and not abusive. Naomi's story engenders hope in us, as she goes from emptiness to fullness in the narrative.

Ruth is about *the coming Messiah.* We find out at the end of the book that Ruth's descendants will be kings of Israel. She is part of the royal line that eventually leads to Jesus.

Note: For the purposes of clarity and conciseness, in each study I have chosen to italicize "Ruth" when referring to the book of *Ruth*, as opposed to the character Ruth, whose name will remain un-italicized.

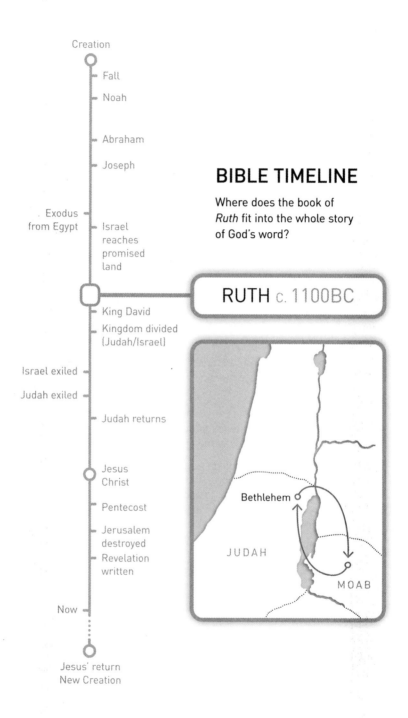

Creation

Fall

Noah

Abraham

Joseph

Exodus
from Egypt

Israel
reaches
promised
land

BIBLE TIMELINE

Where does the book of
Ruth fit into the whole story
of God's word?

RUTH c. 1100BC

King David

Kingdom divided
(Judah/Israel)

Israel exiled

Judah exiled

Judah returns

Jesus
Christ

Pentecost

Jerusalem
destroyed

Revelation
written

Now

Bethlehem

JUDAH

MOAB

Jesus' return
New Creation

1

Ruth 1:1-5
LEAVING GOD'S LAND

⊕ talkabout

1. Can you think of any love stories, from real life or fiction, between two unlikely people?

⊥ investigate

▶ Read Ruth 1:1-5

2. Use verses 2 and 4, plus 4:10, to fill in the gaps in Naomi's family tree, below.

   Then cross a line through the names of those people who had died by the end of Ruth 1:5.

_____ *married* Naomi

Mahlon   *married* _____   _____ *married* _____

3. When and where does the book of *Ruth* start (v 1)?

- What was the immediate problem, and what did Elimelech do as a result (v 1)?

- What was Elimelech aiming to do in Moab (Ruth 1:1)? What did he and his family actually do (v 2 and 4)?

4. Other Old Testament books help us to understand the background to this story. **Read Judges 21:25.** What were the people of Israel like at this time?

- In Deuteronomy 28, God promises blessing on his people for obedience, but warned them of curses for disobedience. Those curses included famine (Deuteronomy 28:18, 38-40). How were God's people to respond (see Deuteronomy 30:2-3, 8-10)?

5. The Hebrew names in the book of *Ruth* have specific and relevant meanings: Bethlehem = "house of bread"; Elimelech = "my God is king"; Naomi = "sweet". At the beginning of this story, neither Bethlehem nor Elimelech live up to their names. In what way?

optional

Moab was a long-standing enemy of Israel. **Read Genesis 19:30-38, Numbers 25:1-9 and Judges 3:12-14** to find out more about Moab.

How did the Moabite nation begin (Genesis 19:37)?

How did the Moabites tempt God's people to sin (Numbers 25:1-3)?

How did Eglon, the king of Moab, treat the Israelites (Judges 3:14)?

⊖ **apply**

6. Can you think of some examples of people nowadays doing what's right in their own eyes?

- When are you put under pressure to join them, rather than to live God's way?

⊡ **getting personal**

When are you tempted to keep quiet when you see people in your friendship groups, or in the news, living their own way rather than God's way? Pray for an opportunity in the coming week to speak up when you see people "doing what is right in their own eyes."

⊍ **investigate**

▶ **Read Ruth 1:6 and 4:17**

DICTIONARY

LORD (v 6): the way most English Bibles translate "Yahweh": the personal name of God (see Exodus 3:13-15).

7. Up to this point Naomi's story is one of tragedy and suffering. What hint of a better future did Naomi hear (1:6)?

• How did she respond?

8. Naomi didn't know how her story would end, but the Lord did. Who was going to be born into Naomi's family (4:17)? And who else (see Matthew 1:1)?

➡ apply

9. We don't know how our own stories will end, but the Lord does! **Read 1 Peter 1:3-4.** What is the future inheritance for all those who are in Christ? How certain is it?

<table>
<tr><td>**DICTIONARY**</td></tr>
<tr><td>**Imperishable (v 4):** unable to rot or die.
Undefiled (v 4): clean, pure.</td></tr>
</table>

10. How does this make a difference to how you see the coming week, month, and year?

getting personal

When is it hardest for you to trust God's plan for your life? What will you do to remind yourself this week that he is sovereign over all things?

⬆ **pray**

God moves in a mysterious way
His wonders to perform;
He plants his footsteps in the sea
And rides upon the storm.

Ye fearful Saints, fresh courage take;
The clouds ye so much dread
Are big with mercy and shall break
In blessings on your head.

His purposes will ripen fast,
Unfolding ev'ry hour;
The bud may have a bitter taste,
But sweet will be the flower.

Blind unbelief is sure to err
And scan his works in vain;
God is his own interpreter,
And he will make it plain. (William Cowper, 1731-1800)

Take some of the lines in this hymn and turn them into prayer.

2 Ruth 1:6-22
THE RETURN

The story so far

In the days when the judges ruled, an Israelite family moved to Moab to avoid the famine in Judah. Elimelech did what was right in his own eyes.

⊕ talkabout

1. What good news have you heard recently, and how did you hear it?

⬇ investigate

> ❱ **Read Ruth 1:6-18**

2. For the first time in the book of *Ruth*, we read good news. What is it (v 6)?

DICTIONARY

Refrain (v 13): stop yourself from doing something.

• What evidence of God's grace do we see in verse 6?

3. Naomi encourages Ruth and Orpah to return to Moab. How do they initially respond (v 10)?

• What reasons does Naomi give for them to return to their home country (v 8-13)?

• How do Ruth and Orpah then respond (v 14-15)?

Ruth's reply to Naomi is written in a Hebrew form known as a chiasm. This pattern is clear when verses 16-17 are printed like this:

"Do not urge me to leave you or to return from following you.
　For where you go I will go, and where you lodge I will lodge.
　　Your people shall be my people, and your God my God.
　Where you die I will die, and there will I be buried.
May the Lord do so to me and more also if anything but death parts me from you."

4. With a chiasm, the outer statements echo one another, and the central statement is the most important point. So what is the core statement that Ruth is making here?

• What is Ruth committing herself to in verses 16-17?

⊝ apply

5. Ruth has counted the cost of following the Lord, and has committed herself to doing what it takes. When have you most recently had to count the cost of being a Christian?

• What will it look like this week to turn from the expectations of a sinful world and instead delight in living for the Lord?

⊡ getting personal

What is the cost of living as a Christian that you personally find the hardest? Who will you ask to help you live for Christ in this area? (A mature Christian friend? Your small-group leader?)

⊌ investigate

▶ **Read Ruth 1:19-22**

DICTIONARY

Mara (v 20): bitter.
Testify (v 21): speak or give evidence.
Calamity (v 21): disaster.

6. How did people react when Naomi and Ruth arrived in Bethlehem (v 19)? Why do you think this might have been?

• What name does Naomi choose for herself and why (v 20)?

• What else does Naomi say about God (v 21)?

7. Do you think that Naomi's accusations against God were valid? Why or why not?

The name "Mara" (or "Marah") has a rich history. When God's people rebelled in the wilderness, Mara was the name of the place where they grumbled against him.

> ❯ **Read Exodus 15:22-27**

What did the Israelites grumble about, and how did God answer Moses' prayer (v 24-25)?

Where did the Lord then take the people (v 27)?

When Naomi called herself "Mara", how would she have been helped if she paused to reflect on Israel's experience at Mara?

8. What sign of God's grace appears at the very end of chapter 1?

⊝ **apply**

9. Like Naomi, we may want to call ourselves "Mara" at times. When we feel this way, how can we remind ourselves of the Lord's grace?

10. What sign of God's grace have you seen in your church family recently?

• Do you find it harder to spot graces than problems, do you think? Why or why not?

⊡ getting personal

Naomi's speeches in verses 8-13 show that there is no earthly reason for Ruth to put her trust in the Lord; yet she does. As with every person who comes to faith, the conversion is God's work. Ruth was chosen by God before the foundation of the world (Ephesians 1:4).

If you're a Christian, then God chose you, too, before the world even existed. How will that perspective affect how you see yourself this week? If you're not sure you're a Christian, who will you talk to about how you can know the Lord personally yourself?

⊡ pray

Use your answers to question 10a to praise God for his good provision for your church family.

Then ask for further signs of his grace as you look ahead to any concerns that are coming up.

3 Ruth 2:1-13
A FIELD OF FAVOR

The story so far

The Israelite Elimelech and his family moved to Moab to avoid the famine in Judah, but Elimelech and his two sons died in Moab.

After hearing that the Lord had blessed Judah with a harvest, Naomi and Ruth returned to Bethlehem. But Naomi now called herself "Mara", meaning bitter.

⟷ talkabout

1. What do the phrases "a worthy man" or "a man of standing" make you think of?

    •➔ Who would you apply this phrase to (either from history or someone alive today)?

⬇ investigate

> **Read Ruth 2:1-13**

2. What do we learn about Boaz in verse 1?

> **DICTIONARY**
>
> **Glean (v 7):** gather leftover grain from a harvested field.
> **Sheaves (v 7):** bundles of harvested barley stalks.
> **Reapers (v 7):** harvesters.
> **Vessels (v 9):** pots.

• What do verses 3, 4 and 11 add to this picture of Boaz?

3. What does Ruth plan to do in verse 2? (See also Ruth 1:22.)

• How does Naomi respond to Ruth's plan (v 2)?

• How hard does Ruth work (v 7; see also v 17)?

4. **Read Judges 21:25.** How do Boaz and Ruth compare to most people in the days of the Judges?

🔅 **explore more**

optional

▶ **Read Deuteronomy 24:19-22 and Leviticus 19:9-10**

What are the harvesters told to do and why?

Who is allowed to glean in the fields?

5. How does Boaz provide for Ruth (v 8-9)?

• Why (v 10-11)?

⤳ apply

6. Ruth is overwhelmed by the grace she receives from Boaz. How does her response in verse 10 point us to how we can respond to the grace God has shown us?

• **Read Ephesians 2:8-9.** As Christians, why have we "found favor" in God's eyes?

⊡ getting personal

Think back to how the Lord brought you to know and trust him. Can you remember a specific moment of conversion? Or did it feel like a gradual process? How could you tell a non-Christian about it so that the focus is on God's grace, not on anything you did or achieved?

⊕ investigate

❯ Re-read Ruth 2:10-13

7. In addition to providing for Ruth, Boaz blesses her with his words. What does Boaz say to Ruth in verses 11-12:

• about her?

• about God?

• about what he's praying?

8. How does this make Ruth feel (v 13)?

In the book of Micah we read the following:

"He has told you, O man, what is good;
    and what does the LORD require of you
but to do justice, and to love kindness,
    and to walk humbly with your God?" (Micah 6:8)

9. How do we see Boaz living out this verse in Ruth 2:1-13?

⇥ apply

10. What would someone in your church family who lived out Micah 6:8 be doing with their time and money?

⊡ getting personal

Read Micah 6:8 again. How can you live this out yourself in the coming week?

⬆ pray

"The LORD ... under whose wings you have come to take refuge."

(Ruth 2:12)

For yourself: What do you want to say now to God, who shelters you under his wings?

For others: Pray for someone known to you who doesn't yet know and love the Lord. Pray that God will draw them under his caring wings soon. Ask God to show you how you can be a part of that change.

4 Ruth 2:14-23
HOSPITALITY, KINDNESS, AND HOPE

The story so far

The Israelite Elimelech and his family moved to Moab to avoid the famine in Judah, but Elimelech and his two sons died in Moab.

After hearing that the Lord had blessed Judah with a harvest, Naomi and Ruth returned to Bethlehem. But Naomi now called herself "Mara", meaning bitter.

Ruth gleaned for barley in Boaz's field. Boaz is a model of justice and grace—and a picture of Christ.

⊕ talkabout

1. When were you last invited to join someone for a meal? How did they show you that you were welcome?

   • Have you ever been to a meal where you weren't made welcome? What was that like? How did you feel?

⊕ investigate

▶ **Read Ruth 2:14-23**

2. Think back to the previous study. What did you discover about Boaz's character?

- What does Boaz do in verses 14-16 that matches what you already know about him?

- What was the result for Ruth (v 17-18)?

3. Naomi had a lot to say when Ruth came home (v 19-22). What questions did Naomi ask?

- What did Naomi then say about Boaz?

4. Do you find the end of chapter 2 encouraging or discouraging, and why?

5. Verse 14 shows us Boaz's hospitality at the mealtime. What do we learn about Boaz from this scene?

↑ pray

Now would be a great moment to pray. It is hard for many of us to adequately appreciate having enough food to satisfy our needs. But to a poor, desperate widow, this meal would have been wonderful. We should pause, thank God for our daily bread, and ask him to use us to bless those who are in need—not only materially, but also relationally with an attitude of warmth.

→ apply

6. Meals with others are about more than food. How can you apply Boaz's example to meals with your church family, with your neighbors, and with your own family?

⊡ getting personal

Many people eat most or all of their meals on their own. If that's you, what change might you be able to make so that you eat one meal this week with someone else? Or, if you regularly eat with others, how will you include someone who is often alone?

↓ investigate

The concept of redemption is central to the Bible. In *Ruth*, and across the biblical storyline, we see 1) the need for redemption, 2) the price of redemption, 3) the nature of the redeemer, and 4) the familial nature of redemption.

7. *NEED:* Fill in the table on the next page to show some of the reasons why the New Testament says we need to be redeemed.

Passage	Why we are helpless	What we need
Romans 6:17-18	Slaves to sin	
Ephesians 2:12-13	Alienated from God	
Colossians 1:13-14		To be transferred to the Son's kingdom of light
John 10:11		Rescue by the Good Shepherd

- It has been said that, to become a Christian, "all you need is need." What do you think this means?

8. *PRICE:* We will see the price of redeeming Ruth and Naomi in *Ruth* 3 – 4. What does the New Testament say about the price of redeeming us in 1 Corinthians 6:20 and 1 Peter 1:18-19?

9. *NATURE:* To be a redeemer you have to have both the willingness and the ability to redeem. As we will see, Boaz had both. How does Philippians 2:6-8 show Jesus' willingness to redeem?

• How does Jesus' ability to redeem exceed that of Boaz (see Revelation 5:9)?

10. *FAMILY:* **Read Galatians 4:4-7.** What familial image is used to describe what it is like to be redeemed by Christ?

⊡ **explore more**

optional

Look up some other examples where redemption is linked with loving or familial language:

• Deuteronomy 7:6-8

• Isaiah 54:5

• Isaiah 63:16

⊖ **apply**

When we look at Boaz, we see many godly traits to imitate. But when we look through Boaz, we see the gospel of Jesus Christ.

11. Think of one or more non-Christians you want to share the gospel with. At this moment, do they most need to understand their need of redemption, the price it cost, the nature of Jesus the Redeemer, or the family they would be redeemed into?

How will you make an opportunity to share this with them this week or this month?

⬆ pray

"But when the fullness of time had come, God sent forth his Son, born of woman, born under the law, to redeem those who were under the law, so that we might receive adoption as sons. And because you are sons, God has sent the Spirit of his Son into our hearts, crying, 'Abba! Father!'" (Galatians 4:4-6)

If we are in Christ, we are adopted into God's family. How does that make you feel? Turn those thoughts into prayers of thanks and praise. Then pray for those whose names you wrote down in question 11.

5 Ruth 3:1-18
COLD FEET

The story so far

The Israelite Elimelech and his family moved to Moab to avoid a famine. Ten years later, his widow Naomi and daughter-in-law Ruth returned to Bethlehem.

Ruth gleaned for barley in Boaz's field. Boaz was a model of justice and grace—and a picture of Jesus Christ.

Boaz showed Ruth and Naomi hospitality and generosity, and was revealed as being a possible redeemer for them.

⊕ talkabout

1. If you're married, who proposed and how? Do you know any stories about unusual marriage proposals?

⊕ investigate

> **Read Ruth 3:1-6**

2. Who initiated Ruth's meeting with Boaz?

DICTIONARY

Winnow (v 2): blow away unwanted husks from grain.
Threshing floor (v 3): a special flattened floor used to beat out and winnow grain.
Anoint (v 3): pour over.

3. Naomi could have said "God is sovereign, so let's just wait until a husband knocks on the door." Why do you think she didn't do that?

4. Naomi provides specific instructions for Ruth (v 3-4). What are the seven steps she proposes?

1. Wash...

2. Put on...

3. Put on...

4. Visit...

5. Observe...

6. Uncover...

7. Listen...

5. How does Ruth respond to Naomi's plan (v 5)?

➡ **apply**

This risky strategy depends on the kindness, the integrity, and the status as a kinsman-redeemer, of Boaz. For us, too, there is one person on whom everything depends: the Lord Jesus.

6. How is Jesus the "perfect Boaz"?

• What risks can Christians take because of the kindness, integrity, and redeeming power of Jesus?

⬇ **investigate**

▶ **Read Ruth 3:7-18**

7. Does Ruth follow Naomi's plan exactly? Compare verse 4 with verse 9.

DICTIONARY

Garment (v 15): piece of clothing.

• How does Boaz respond to Ruth's request (v 10-11)?

- How does this relate to what we already know of Boaz's character?

- What is the possible hitch in the plan (v 12)?

8. **Read Deuteronomy 25:5-10.** If a married man died without having a son to carry on the family name, what was his brother obligated to do?

- If he refused, how was his brother's widow able to get justice (v 7)?

- Does this ruling about the duties of a kinsman-redeemer apply to Boaz?

⊡ **explore more**

optional

❯ **Read Proverbs 31:10-31**

The book of Ruth allows us to see an example of what a Proverbs 31 woman looks like in an ungodly culture. What similarities can you see?

9. Ruth returns to Naomi with six measures of barley (60-90 pounds / 30-40kg of grain). What extra information does Ruth tell her mother-in-law, and how does Naomi respond (Ruth 3:17-18)?

☺ getting personal

Previously, Naomi told Ruth to act (v 1-5). Now she tells her to rest in the work of Boaz (v 18). She believes Boaz to be a man of his word, who will not leave important work unfinished.

Are you known as a man or woman of your word? What forthcoming opportunities do you have to be as trustworthy as Boaz?

→ apply

Sometimes, when we read a Bible story, it gives us a direct example to follow. But *Ruth* 3 contains much that we cannot imitate, such as threshing-floor marriage proposals!

10. Think again about the actions of Naomi, Ruth and Boaz in this chapter. How can you apply their example to your own lives this week?

↑ pray

Jesus Christ, our Redeemer, has changed everything. He has changed our status, brought us into intimate union with himself, and given us glorious hope for the future. Praise and thank him for these things.

6 Ruth 4:1-12
TAKE MY SANDAL

The story so far

When the widowed Naomi and her daughter-in-law Ruth returned to Israel from Moab, Ruth gleaned for barley in Boaz's field.

Boaz was a redeemer who showed hospitality and generosity, and who gave Ruth and Naomi hope. He points forward to Christ as our Redeemer.

Naomi devised a plan; it led to Ruth's proposal to Boaz. Boaz responded with a promise to Ruth, and by providing for her.

⊕ talkabout

1. What procedures have you needed to follow to make any legal transactions or agreements (such as buying a house or car, or getting married)?

⬇ investigate

> **Read Ruth 4:1-12**

2. Verses 1-12 all happen at the city gate. Imagine that you are filming these verses for television. How might you break the events up into a series of different scenes?

> **DICTIONARY**
>
> **Behold (v 1):** look, observe.
> **Elders (v 2):** senior figures.
> **Parcel of land (v 3):** field or set of fields.
> **Impair (v 6):** harm.
> **Redemption (v 6):** buying back.
> **Attest (v 7):** certify or confirm a legal transaction.

3. Compare Ruth 2:4, 3:8 and 4:1. How does the author of *Ruth* use "and behold" within this book?

4. How does the other redeemer respond to Boaz's initial suggestion (v 4)? What changes in verse 6 and why?

- This other redeemer is never named in the narrative. Why do you think that might be?

➔ apply

When the other redeemer was given the option of buying land that would bring profit to him and his family, he was keen to do so. But he changed his mind when he heard about marrying Ruth, saying "I cannot redeem it for myself, lest I impair my own inheritance" (v 6).

5. Can you think of examples from your church family where someone has acted in a godly way even though it has cost them financially or personally to do so?

⊡ getting personal

Have you ever refused to help someone because the cost was too much? If so, admit this to God and ask him to help you to do better next time. Is there a friend, neighbor, or family member you could help this week, no matter what it costs you?

⊕ investigate

> ❯ **Re-read Ruth 4:7-12**

6. How did the other redeemer confirm the transaction with Boaz, and who witnessed it?

• What did Boaz redeem on that day?

7. Compare the other redeemer with Boaz. What do they have in common? How are they different?

• What do you think the priorities are for each man?

8. A true redeemer is willing to pay a price for the good of others. How is this true of Boaz? How is Jesus Christ the ultimate Kinsman-Redeemer?

⊡ **explore more**

optional

❯ **Read Philippians 2:1-11**

How do verses 6-11 show Jesus acting as our Kinsman-Redeemer?

How do verses 1-5 match the character and actions of Boaz?

9. One more significant thing happens at the city gate: a three-fold prayer of blessing from the people and the elders. What are the three blessings (Ruth 4:11-12)?

• How were these prayers answered?

⤷ apply

10. How has this study helped your appreciation of the character and love of Jesus your Redeemer to grow? What aspect of Jesus' character do you most want to hold on to this week?

⊡ getting personal

We must never lose the wonder of our Redeemer's love for us, displayed most fully at the cross. Do you know this love? If you're not sure, who can you talk to about it this week? If you do know it, who can you tell about his love this week?

⬆ pray

"Redeeming love has been my theme,
And shall be till I die."
(William Cowper, *There Is a Fountain Filled with Blood*)

Spend some time thinking about the redeeming love of Jesus. Thank him. Praise him. Ask him to give you opportunities to tell others about his love.

7

Ruth 4:13-22
THE PROMISED SON

The story so far

Boaz was a redeemer who showed hospitality and generosity, and who gave Ruth and Naomi hope. He points forward to Christ as our Redeemer.

Naomi devised a plan; it led to Ruth's proposal to Boaz. Boaz responded with a promise to Ruth, and by providing for her.

Redeeming Ruth was not straightforward: there was a price to pay. Only Boaz was willing to pay it.

⊕ talkabout

1. Do you know any children who show a strong family likeness with one of their parents? It could be a visual likeness, a similar character trait, the same laugh or smile…

⊕ investigate

❯ **Read Ruth 4:13-22**

2. In study 1 (page 7) we created Ruth's family tree. Now use verses 21-22 to fill in the next few generations in the tree on the following page. If you're not sure of the final name, check Matthew 1:17.

DICTIONARY

Went in to her (v 13): slept with her.
Renowned (v 14): famous.

```
          Elimelech   married   Naomi
               │
    ┌──────────┴───────────────────────────────┐
    │                                           │
  Mahlon  married    Ruth    married _____   Chilion  married  Orpah
                              ┬
                           ___│___
                              ┬
                           ___│___
                              ┬
                              ┆   Approx 1,000
                              ┆   years later
                              ┆
                          _____
```

3. In Ruth 4:13-22 we see that God provides a son for Boaz and Ruth, a redeemer for Naomi, a king for Israel, and the Messiah for the world. Which verse matches each of these four gifts from God?

• A son for Boaz and Ruth

• A redeemer for Naomi

• A king for Israel

• The Messiah for the world (see also Matthew 1:1)

4. How has Ruth's status changed from Ruth 1 to Ruth 4? (See Ruth 1:4-5, 22; 2:10, 13; 3:9; 4:13.)

⊡ **explore more**

optional

Throughout the biblical narrative, God intervenes in order to bring forth children who are significant in redemptive history. Often these children are born of women who were previously childless— something which highlights the fact that it is the Lord who provides these births. Investigate one or more of their stories:

• Sarah (Genesis 18:10-15; 21:1-7)

• Rebecca (Genesis 25:21-26)

• Rachel and Leah (Genesis 29:31-35, 30:22-24)

• Hannah (1 Samuel 1:10-11, 19-20)

How is Ruth's story similar to theirs?

5. In Ruth 1, we saw how Naomi changed her name. What did she change it to and why (Ruth 1:20-21)?

• How have things changed for Naomi by Ruth 4:14-17?

- What did the women say Ruth's child would do for Naomi (v 15)? Why do you think they were confident of this?

⊡ apply

6. The women were confident that Obed would have a similar character to his mother, Ruth. As Christians, we have God as our loving Father and Jesus as our rescuing Brother. How have you seen your own character changing to show more of a family likeness with your Father and Brother?

⊡ getting personal

The fruit of the Spirit, working in our lives, is "love, joy, peace, patience, kindness, goodness, faithfulness, gentleness, self-control" (Galatians 5:22-23). This is also the character of Jesus. What aspect of this fruit do you want to grow more of? What actions will you take to help with this?

⊡ investigate

> ❯ Read Judges 21:25 and Ruth 1:1

7. What was the historical background to the book of *Ruth*?

• Why does this make the last few verses of Ruth 4 so important?

▶ Read Matthew 1:1-6a

8. How are verses 3b-6a similar to Ruth 4:18-22?

DICTIONARY

Genealogy (v 1):
family line of descent.
Messiah/Christ (v 1):
anointed one; God's
chosen King.

• Women were not usually included in genealogies, since descent was traced through the men. Which women have been included in Jesus' genealogy? (See also Matthew 1:3a, 6b, 16.)

• These women included a prostitute, a Moabite, and an adulterer. Why is it surprising that these women are in Jesus' family tree? What does it teach us about the people God uses to work his purposes out?

9. In Ruth 4:14-15 we read that Obed was going to be a "redeemer," "a restorer of life and a nourisher of ... old age." Matthew 1 tells us how an even more significant son was born in Bethlehem. How was Jesus even better than Obed? (See Matthew 1:21-23.)

⭢ apply

10. Think back over the book of *Ruth*. How has it pointed you to Jesus? What have you been most helped by? What challenge will you take away with you?

⬆ pray

For Christians there is an even greater resolution than the one experienced by Naomi. For us, there is no need for bitterness over our circumstances and no reason to compromise in our obedience. We live in the light of the glorious birth of Jesus. We rejoice in the saving grace of Jesus. We rest in the already-not-yet peace of Jesus: Ruth and Boaz's descendant and the church's great Redeemer.

Turn some of these thoughts into prayer.

The Lord
provides

LEADER'S GUIDE

Leader's Guide

INTRODUCTION

Leading a Bible study can be a bit like herding cats—everyone has a different idea of what the passage could be about, and a different line of enquiry that they want to pursue. But a good group leader is more than someone who just referees this kind of discussion. You will want to:

- correctly understand and handle the Bible passage. But also…

- encourage and train the people in your group to do this for themselves. Don't fall into the trap of spoon-feeding people by simply passing on the information in the Leader's Guide. Then…

- make sure that no Bible study is finished without everyone knowing how the passage is relevant for them. What changes do you all need to make in the light of the things you have been learning? And finally…

- encourage the group to turn all that has been learned and discussed into prayer.

Your Bible-study group is unique, and you are likely to know better than anyone the capabilities, backgrounds and circumstances of the people you are leading. That's why we've designed these guides with a number of optional features. If they're a quiet bunch, you might want to spend longer on *talkabout*. If your time is limited, you can choose to skip *explore more*, or get people to look at these questions at home. Can't get enough of Bible study? Well, some studies have optional extra homework projects. As leader, you can adapt and select the material to the needs of your particular group.

So what's in the Leader's Guide? The main thing that this Leader's Guide will help you to do is to understand the major teaching points in the passage you are studying, and how to apply them. As well as guidance for the questions, the Leader's Guide for each session contains the following important sections:

THE BIG IDEA

One or two key sentences will give you the main point of the session. This is what you should be aiming to have fixed in people's minds as they leave the Bible study. And it's the point you need to head back toward when the discussion goes off at a tangent.

SUMMARY

An overview of the passage, including plenty of useful historical background information.

OPTIONAL EXTRA

Usually this is an introductory activity that ties in with the main theme of the Bible study, and is designed to "break the ice" at the beginning of a session. Or it may be a "homework project" that people can tackle during the week.

So let's take a look at the various different features of a Good Book Guide:

⊕ talkabout

Each session kicks off with a discussion question, based on the group's opinions or experiences. It's designed to get people talking and thinking in a general way about the main subject of the Bible study.

⬇ investigate

The first thing you and your group need to know is what the Bible passage is about, which is the purpose of these questions. But watch out—people may come up with answers based on their experiences or teaching they have heard in the past, without referring to the passage at all. It's amazing how often we can get through a Bible study without actually looking at the Bible! If you're stuck for an answer, the Leader's Guide contains guidance for questions. These are the answers to direct your group to. This information isn't meant to be read out to people—ideally, you want them to discover these answers from the Bible for themselves. Sometimes there are optional follow-up questions (see ⊗ in guidance for questions) to help you help your group get to the answer.

⬒ explore more

These questions generally point people to other relevant parts of the Bible. They are useful for helping your group to see how the passage fits into the "big picture" of the whole Bible. These sections are OPTIONAL—only use them if you have time. Remember that it's better to finish in good time having really grasped one big thing from the passage, than to try and cram everything in.

→ apply

We want to encourage you to spend more time working at application—too often, it is simply tacked on at the end. In the Good Book Guides, apply sections are mixed in with the investigate sections of the study. We hope that people will realize that application is not just an optional extra, but rather, the whole purpose of studying the

Bible. We do Bible study so that our lives can be changed by what we hear from God's word. If you skip the application, the Bible study hasn't achieved its purpose.

These questions draw out practical lessons that we can all learn from the Bible passage. You can review what has been learned so far, and think about practical differences that this should make in our churches and our lives. The group gets the opportunity to talk about what they personally have learned.

☺ getting personal

These can be done at home, but it is well worth allowing a few moments of quiet reflection during the study for each person to think and pray about specific changes they need to make in their own lives. Why not have a time for reporting back at the beginning of the following session, so that everyone can be encouraged and challenged by one another to make application a priority?

⬆ pray

In Acts 4:25-30 the first Christians quoted Psalm 2 as they prayed in response to the persecution of the apostles by the Jewish religious leaders. Today however, it's not as common for Christians to base prayers on the truths of God's word as it once was. As a result, our prayers tend to be weak, superficial and self-centered rather than bold, visionary and God-centered.

The prayer section is based on what has been learned from the Bible passage. How different our prayer times would be if we were genuinely responding to what God has said to us through his word.

1 Ruth 1:1-5
LEAVING GOD'S LAND

THE BIG IDEA

Ruth's story begins "in the days when the judges ruled" (Ruth 1:1), and we see an Israelite family moving to Moab to avoid the famine in Judah. Like the people of his day, Elimelech did what was right in his own eyes (Judges 21:25).

SUMMARY

Ruth opens with some devastating words. The first time I read the opening five verses of Ruth to my children and explained the names of the characters and a bit of the background, they were shocked and perplexed. Things go from bad to worse.

Coming after the book of Judges, which displays the problems of Israel on a broader national and local level, Ruth zooms in on one particular family's trials and tragedies. It takes place during the time in which "the judges ruled" (v 1), which was a period of spiritual darkness. We also read of a "famine" in the land (v 1), likely a sign of judgment. And things get even worse, as we read of three funerals. Within a few verses we are left with a grieving widow in a foreign land, with her two widowed daughters-in-law (v 3-5).

But the immediate suffering of this family is not the only thing we need to notice. The central focus of Ruth actually concerns the origins of Israel's royal line. The genealogy that appears at the end of Ruth clarifies this issue (4:18-22). The crisis introduced here in 1:1-5 involves the widowhood of Naomi and Ruth, meaning the family line is threatened. But the genealogy shows us that Obed, whose birth solves the crisis

and continues the family line, will be the grandfather of David, Israel's greatest king. God had promised to send a king to Israel to rule on God's behalf (Genesis 17:6; 35:11; 49:10). In Judges, this is threatened because of widespread unfaithfulness. In Ruth, that threat begins to be solved.

There is a hint of all of this in Ruth 1:1, as we read of Elimelech's "Ephrathite" lineage. This was a name for those whose families were from Bethlehem. The book's first readers might have known that David was of this line—a link we read about in 1 Samuel 17:12.

The book of Ruth takes place during one of the darkest periods in Israel's history: the days of the judges. The period of the judges came after the land was settled, and before the monarchy was established. During this time there was no national government. Israel was a collection of tribes. These judges were local "chieftains" that were called to overthrow foreign oppressors. They were local military leaders, not national political leaders.

It was a period filled with violence, idolatry, moral depravity, and civil war. The following words are repeated in the book of Judges and are the final line we read in the book: "There was no king in Israel. Everyone did what was right in his own eyes" (Judges 21:25; see also 17:6; 18:1; 19:1). It is against this black backdrop that Boaz and Ruth shine. It is somewhat surprising to find godly examples in this time period! Further, it is in this dark season that the providence of God shines. Despite sin and rebellion, God is working out his redemptive purposes.

It is in this kind of context that Christians are called to shine. Ruth and Boaz inspire us to do so. The nobility and courage of Ruth and the compassion and righteousness of Boaz will dazzle us. When we put their actions in the context of the judges, then it motivates us to go against the customs of our own day and follow Christ instead.

At this stage in *Ruth*, we have not yet heard how Naomi will respond to the loss of her husband and sons. But in this book we will learn the same lesson of hope that we see throughout Scripture. During Naomi's time of darkness, God is working out his sovereign and saving purposes. We do not always understand what God is doing. But God is at work in the details of our lives too.

OPTIONAL EXTRA

Check online, or use a book of baby names, to discover what your names mean. In biblical times, names were often chosen for their meanings. In the book of *Ruth*, we'll see that the meanings of some names add an extra level to our understanding of the story.

GUIDANCE FOR QUESTIONS

1. Can you think of any love stories, from real life or fiction, between two unlikely people? Examples from fiction might include: a young woman and a terrifying monster in *Beauty and the Beast*; a failed nun and a military captain in *The Sound of Music*; a roughneck cowboy and a classy nurse in *Open Range*; a real-estate stager and an Irish innkeeper in *Leap Year;* and a human and vampire in *Twilight!* Tell your group that this is the sort of story they will meet in *Ruth*. Here, two very unlikely people get together, an Israelite gentleman and a Moabite widow—and she ends up being one of the many-times-great grandmothers of Jesus.

2. Use [Ruth 1] verses 2 and 4, plus Ruth 4:10, to fill in the gaps in Naomi's family tree. Then cross a line through the names of those people who had died by the end of Ruth 1:5. See family tree at bottom of the page.

3. When and where does the book of Ruth start (v 1)? It starts "in the days when the judges ruled", and in the town of Bethlehem, which is in Judah (the southern part of Israel).

- **What was the immediate problem, and what did Elimelech do as a result (v 1)?** There was famine in Israel, so Elimelech took his wife and two sons and moved to the country of Moab.

- **What was Elimelech aiming to do in Moab (Ruth 1:1)? What did he and his family actually do (v 2 and 4)?** They were aiming "to sojourn"—to live for a while—in Moab (v 1); but instead they "remained there" (v 2) for ten years (v 4).

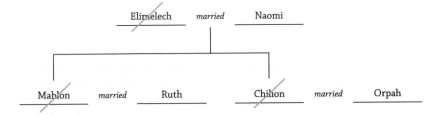

4. Other Old Testament books help us to understand the background to this story. Read Judges 21:25. What were the people of Israel like at this time? Judges 21:25 tells us that "In those days there was no king in Israel. Everyone did what was right in his own eyes."

- **In Deuteronomy 28, God promises blessing on his people for obedience, but warned them of curses for disobedience. Those curses included famine (Deuteronomy 28:18, 38-40). How were God's people to respond (see Deuteronomy 30:2-3, 8-10)?** God promised blessing on his people for obedience, but warned them of curses for disobedience, which included infertility, defeat, and famine (Deuteronomy 28:15-68). Due to Israel's disobedience, during the time of Ruth, God's word came true. The fields were barren, and the crops failed. The barns were empty.

This famine should have led the people to repent. God promised that he would lift the curse, should they do so (Deuteronomy 30:2-3, 8-10).

5. The Hebrew names in the book of *Ruth* have specific and relevant meanings: Bethlehem = "house of bread"; Elimelech = "my God is king"; Naomi = "sweet". At the beginning of this story, neither Bethlehem nor Elimelech live up to their names. In what way? There was famine in Bethlehem, meaning there was no bread in the "house of bread".

Elimelech acted like the people of his day and did what was right in his own eyes. The appropriate response to the famine would have been to remain in Israel, to repent, to call others to repent, and to trust God. But it seems he felt more at home in the land

of compromise than the land of promise. Instead of repenting, he takes matters into his own hands (Ruth 1:2). Elimelech, whose name means, "My God is King," does not act like his God is king. Sinclair Ferguson says: "Instead of turning back to the Lord, they turned their backs on the Lord, and go to live in Moab" (*Faithful God*, p 24). Instead of mourning over the sin of the land and asking God to restore things, Elimelech leaves the fields of Bethlehem for the fields of Moab.

EXPLORE MORE

... How did the Moabite nation begin (Genesis 19:37)? Moab, which lay on the other side of the Dead Sea, was an interesting choice of destination for Elimelech and his family. The Moabites traced their origin back to the incestuous relationship between Lot and his oldest daughter (Genesis 19:30-38).

How did the Moabites tempt God's people to sin (Numbers 25:1-3, 9)? The king of Moab, Balak, hired the prophet Balaam to curse Israel (Numbers 22), and the Moabite people began to seduce Israelites into sin by inviting them to participate in false worship and sexual immorality. As a result, the Lord slew 24,000 Israelites (Numbers 25:9).

How did Eglon, the king of Moab, treat the Israelites (Judges 3:14)? He had oppressed Israel.

In going to Moab, Elimelech and his family were certainly turning their back on the Lord and his people.

6. APPLY: Can you think of some examples of people nowadays doing what's right in their own eyes? Answers will vary, but most weeks the news contains several examples of people or governments making choices that go against what the Bible says.

• **When are you put under pressure to join them, rather than to live God's way?** Be ready to give your own answer to start this discussion if no one else says anything.

7. Up to this point Naomi's story is one of tragedy and suffering. What hint of a better future did Naomi hear (1:6)? Even though she was far away in Moab, Naomi heard news from home. She heard that "the LORD had visited his people and given them food" (v 6).

• **How did she respond?** In response, Naomi "arose with her daughters-in-law to return from the country of Moab". She was heading home.

8. Naomi didn't know how her story would end, but the Lord did. Who was going to be born into Naomi's family (4:17)? And who else (see Matthew 1:1)? Obed, the son of Ruth and Boaz, was born into Naomi's family (Ruth 4:17). He was her grandson, and he would be the grandfather of King David. Many generations later, Jesus Christ would also be born into this family line (Matthew 1:1).

9. APPLY: We don't know how our own stories will end, but the Lord does! Read 1 Peter 1:3-4. What is the future inheritance for all those who are in Christ? How certain is it? Through the resurrection of Jesus, we have been born again and saved for eternity. This inheritance is "imperishable, undefiled, and unfading" (v 4).

10. APPLY: How does this make a difference to how you see the coming

week, month, and year? Encourage everyone to give at least one answer to this question. Perhaps you could offer to pray for each other during the week, that these truths will really make a difference and help you all to keep going no matter what the week brings.

2 Ruth 1:6-22
THE RETURN

THE BIG IDEA

After hearing that the Lord has blessed Judah with a harvest, Naomi and Ruth leave Moab and return to Bethlehem. Naomi calls herself "Mara", meaning bitter, but even in her bitterness she sees that the Lord is in control.

SUMMARY

The next portion of *Ruth* presents us with three women—Naomi, Ruth, and Orpah—and the crucial decision they face.

We read first of God's gracious provision to his people (Ruth 1:6): the famine is over. A decision must then be made. Should they return to Bethlehem? In this passage, a geographical and spiritual turning point exists. For the story is not merely about turning back to Bethlehem but also about turning back to the Lord in faith.

Upon hearing news of the harvest, Naomi decides to return home. Ruth and Orpah express a desire not only to go with their mother-in-law but to go to her people. This underlines the depth of devotion they had to each other.

This devotion is another hint of God's provision. Naomi compares the way Ruth and Orpah have treated her with the way she hopes God may treat them: "kindly" (v 8). They are reflecting God's *hesed*, his faithful kindness.

After first rejecting Naomi's proposal, Ruth and Orpah now face a decision. Will they forsake all and follow, or turn back to Moab?

After more weeping, Orpah makes the decision to turn back (v 14-15). Ruth, however, clings tightly to her mother-in-law. She has counted the cost and is abandoning everything to journey with Naomi.

Ruth is a picture of risk-taking faith. Her decision to go with Naomi is rooted in her trust in Yahweh. In this crucial moment of decision, we read of Ruth's stunning profession of faith: "Your people shall be my people, and your God my God" (v 16c).

Ruth has counted the cost, and she is following Yahweh and joining his people. Ruth is not pledging something in the future but stating something that she has already done: a faith and identity that she already has. She is saying, *Naomi, because your God is my God, and your people are my people, I will go with you.*

Naomi gets the message, and they turn for Bethlehem.

When Naomi shows up unannounced after ten years away, her presence creates a stir in the town. The women of Bethlehem ask, "Is this Naomi?"

You have to admire the transparency and candor of Naomi. She gives a sharp response: "Do not call me Naomi; call me Mara, for the Almighty has dealt very bitterly with me" (v 20). "Mara" means "bitter," and she insists they call her by that name.

Naomi believes the Lord has made her life bitter. When she left, she was "full", but now he has made her "empty" (Ruth 1:21). Of course, she was not full physically when she left—after all, there was a famine. But she was full with family and security, having a husband and two sons. She had a happy family when she left. But not anymore. She is empty. She has nothing—or at least that is what she thinks. She can only see her poverty, her lack of husband and sons, and her lack of security.

Then we read a word of hope: "they came to Bethlehem at the beginning of barley harvest" (1:22). The physical famine at the beginning of the chapter also illustrated the spiritual famine in Naomi's life, and the grief she experienced. Now there is a new beginning agriculturally. Will it be a new beginning in other ways for these women? Will Ruth find a husband? Will the family line extend? Will this harvest also bring about a harvest of grace in Naomi's life? Will her bitterness be replaced with joyful praise? Will this hopeless lady experience God's surprising grace? Those hearing the story for the first time will perk up with hope, pondering how things may turn out.

OPTIONAL EXTRA

Find a large map or globe. Ask each group member to use these to show the longest journey they have ever made. Then show the journey that Naomi and Ruth make in today's passage, from ancient Moab (east of the Dead Sea) to Bethlehem (west of the Dead Sea). If you search for "Moab" on Wikipedia, you'll find a helpful map.

GUIDANCE FOR QUESTIONS

1. What good news have you heard recently, and how did you hear it? The next section of the book of *Ruth* starts with Naomi, who is still in Moab, hearing good news from Bethlehem.

2. For the first time in the book of *Ruth*, we read good news. What is it (v 6)? Naomi "had heard in the fields of Moab that the LORD had visited his people and given them food". Covenant blessings had returned in the land of promise. God has "visited" his people with food!

• **What evidence of God's grace do we see in verse 6?**
  • First, Naomi "heard" of this good news, even while she was "in the fields of Moab." She had no television, radio, or social media, but somehow the word made its way to the distant fields of Moab, and Naomi responded. The word "heard" is a sign of gracious provision.
  • Second, it was "the LORD" who provided this remarkable gift of grace. This is the first mention of God in *Ruth*. He is doing what he does regularly in Scripture: providing. In this bleak time of history, God opened his hand and provided food for the hungry.
  • Third, grace is expressed in the word "visit." Sometimes this word is used to mean God's judgment, but here it is used to refer to God visiting in blessing. Similarly, throughout redemptive history, this word is used to speak of God's gracious intervention in a crisis (such as in Genesis 21:1 and 1 Samuel 2:21— these verses say that God "visited" Sarah and Hannah (ESV), translated as "was gracious to" in the NIV).
  • Fourth, we see grace in the phrase "his people." The language reflects God's covenantal relationship with them: the agreement that he would be their God, and they would be his people (Exodus 6:7). The fertile land is a statement: God has not forgotten Israel.
  • Finally, we see what God provides for his people: "food". We may be able to list many ways in which God provides, and many things to be thankful for, but we should not forget that he is also the one who provides for our most basic needs.

3. Naomi encourages Ruth and Orpah to return to Moab. How do they initially

respond (v 10)? They both say that they will return to Judah with Naomi.

- **What reasons does Naomi give for them to return to their home country (v 8-13)?**
- Naomi initially says that she hopes the Lord will "deal kindly" with them (v 8), giving them "rest" and new husbands (v 9).
- When Ruth and Orpah say they will stay with Naomi, she makes their prospects with her clear. She is too old to have more sons for them to marry. And even if she did have sons right away, there would be a very long wait until those sons were old enough to marry.
- Naomi then seems to suggest, in verse 13, that Ruth and Orpah may experience the same "bitterness" as Naomi if they go with her to Judah.

- **How do Ruth and Orpah then respond (v 14-15)?**
- After more weeping, Orpah makes the decision to turn back (v 14-15). She concludes that the safer and more sensible route is returning to Moab where she may find a husband. She kisses her mother-in-law goodbye, and then drops off the pages of Scripture.
- Ruth, however, clings tightly to her mother-in-law. The expression carries the idea of deep loyalty, like that of a marriage (see Genesis 2:24). It involves leaving membership in one group and joining another. She has counted the cost and is abandoning everything to journey with Naomi.

4. With a chiasm, the outer statements echo one another, and the central statement is the most important point. So what is the core statement that Ruth is making here? "Your people shall be my people, and your God shall be my God" (v 16b).

- **What is Ruth committing herself to in verses 16-17?** Ruth commits herself to go, lodge, die, and be buried where Naomi is. Ruth doesn't just commit herself to Naomi's God, but also to her community.

5. APPLY: Ruth has counted the cost of following the Lord, and has committed herself to doing what it takes. When have you most recently had to count the cost of being a Christian? Be ready to give an answer of your own to encourage discussion. Examples might include saying no to a new job that would mean always working on a Sunday; choosing not to buy something new so that you can give the money to support mission work; or standing up for a Christian viewpoint when the opposite is being pushed in the media.

- **What will it look like this week to turn from the expectations of a sinful world and instead delight in living for the Lord?** Encourage group members to be realistic and practical in their answers. Ask them to write down something that they can definitely do this week; and then remember to ask at your next session how they got on.

6. How did people react when Naomi and Ruth arrived in Bethlehem (v 19)? Why do you think this might have been?
- Naomi shows up unannounced after ten years away, and her presence creates a stir in the town. This buzz in the town, translated "stir," derives from a word meaning "to throw into disorder, to confuse." The image is of animated conversation in the town. The people of Bethlehem are all talking to one another.

The women ask, "Is this Naomi?"

- Perhaps their disbelief is founded in excitement: they are full of joy at seeing Naomi again. Or maybe they are judgmental and smug, comparing their own newfound prosperity with her unhappiness. It is also possible that the women of the town have heard of all that she has been through and are concerned for her. Perhaps they sympathize with her and pity her.

- Whatever their tone, they can hardly believe that this is the woman they once knew. Naomi has changed. No doubt she has changed physically after ten years. But there was more to the change than the aging we would expect. The women probably asked this question because of her expression, too. Naomi was a lady filled with sorrow. She left as the "pleasant one" but returned grief-stricken. Naomi left in her prime, and she returned old and destitute.

- Naomi had also changed relationally. She had left Bethlehem with a husband and two sons. She returned accompanied by no men, only a widowed Moabite.

- **What name does Naomi choose for herself and why (v 20)?** She chooses the name "Mara", which means "bitter". Naomi claims that "the Almighty has dealt very bitterly with me" (v 20).

- **What else does Naomi say about God (v 21)?** Naomi says that:
  - she "went away full" (meaning when she and her family went to Moab) but that "the LORD has brought [her] back empty."
  - God has "testified" against her (meaning she feels as though the Lord has held her to account at his courtroom). Perhaps she uses this language because deep down she knows that God has a valid accusation against her—but she does not

admit this.
- God has brought "calamity" upon her. She left with a husband and two sons, but has returned with only a Moabite daughter-in-law.

7. Do you think that Naomi's accusations against God were valid? Why or why not?

- Naomi is venting her frustration: she repeats the word "Mara" or "bitter", saying, "the Almighty has dealt very bitterly with me" (v 20). She attributes her pain to God (v 21).

- Naomi believes the Lord has made her life bitter. When she left, she was "full", but now he has made her "empty" (v 21). Of course, she was not full physically when she left—after all, there was a famine. But she was full with family and security, having a husband and two sons. She had a happy family when she left. But not anymore. She is empty. She has nothing— or at least that is what she thinks. She can only see her poverty, her lack of husband and sons, and her lack of security. The structure of the sentence even makes Naomi and the Lord look like enemies. She pits herself against God, even though it is part of God's character to care for widows (Exodus 22:22-23; see also Psalm 68:5; 146:9).

- While Naomi's venting session may be unpleasant to read, we should notice that she is no atheist! She does not blame "chance," nor an impersonal fate, but God himself. She may not be seeing things clearly, and she definitely does not see things completely, but she at least sees God in her situation.

EXPLORE MORE
... Read Exodus 15:22-27. What did the Israelites grumble about, and how did

God answer Moses' prayer (v 24-25)? God's people complained about a lack of provision, specifically no water. When they could not drink the water at Mara because it was bitter, they grumbled. They cried out to the Lord, and he miraculously made the water drinkable and sweet.

Where did the Lord then take the people (v 27)? Not only did the Lord miraculously provide drinkable water, but he also took them to a place of natural rest and beauty: Elim. The writer of Exodus notes the sight of 70 palm trees and springs of water. God took his people to a place of abundance and refreshment.

When Naomi called herself "Mara", how would she have been helped if she paused to reflect on Israel's experience at Mara? If Naomi had paused to reflect on Israel's experience at Mara, that whole event should have brought hope to her (and to all despairing people). In the midst of the desert, the Lord first provided a miracle at Mara and then provided through more ordinary means at Elim. In both cases the Lord transformed his people's experience.

8. What sign of God's grace appears at the very end of chapter 1? Naomi and Ruth arrive in Bethlehem just as the barley harvest is happening. There is no longer famine in Bethlehem, and—as we shall see in chapter 2—the harvest means that Ruth can provide for herself and Naomi.

9. APPLY: Like Naomi, we may want to call ourselves "Mara" at times. When we feel this way, how can we remind ourselves of the Lord's grace? One wonderful way of doing this is to read the stories in the Bible, Old Testament as well as New. Remembering the ways God has worked in the past will help us to get better at being aware of the way God is working in the present. (It would have helped Naomi to remember how the Lord provided for his people at the first "Mara".)

You can also look back in your own lives and remember how God has held you fast in the past, and can therefore be trusted to do the same now.

10. APPLY: What sign of God's grace have you seen in your church family recently? Be ready with an answer of your own if the group struggle to think of anything.

- **Do you find it harder to spot graces than problems, do you think? Why/ why not?** One way to approach this question would be to ask what people talk about after a church service. Are they reminding each other how God has blessed them? Or discussing their latest problems or disappointments with church?

3 Ruth 2:1-13
A FIELD OF FAVOR

THE BIG IDEA
Boaz is a model of justice and grace—and in this way he exemplifies Micah 6:8, is a picture of Christ, and stands as a challenge to us to live in the same way.

SUMMARY
The first chapter of *Ruth* dealt primarily with three women, but now the narrative widens to include the whole community. We are introduced to a "worthy man," Boaz, in the first verse (2:1). It is as if the author is saying, *Keep your eye on this guy!*

As we read *Ruth* 2, we need to keep in mind the darkness of the days of the judges, so that we will be even more impressed by Boaz's integrity, his protection for the vulnerable, and his compassion to the poor. Boaz was different than many of the men of his day. We, too, need a new generation of men like him. These words of the psalmist could be said of Boaz:

"Blessed is the man who fears the LORD, who greatly delights in his commandments! His offspring will be mighty in the land; the generation of the upright will be blessed … It is well with the man who deals generously and lends; who conducts his affairs with justice … He has distributed freely; he has given to the poor; his righteousness endures forever; his horn is exalted in honor." (Psalm 112:1-2; 5, 9).

These are some key marks of godliness. This description certainly reflects the character of Boaz.

But there is more to Boaz than a model of justice: he is also a picture of Christ. So as we look *at* Boaz, we also want to look

through Boaz, so that we may see our Savior. Boaz's grace points to Jesus' grace, the grace that has bought our salvation, the grace that strengthens and empowers us to love this broken world. Jesus, in his kindness, has sought the outcast, has given us refuge, has fed us at his table, and has become our Redeemer. Now in Christ we have a new status and are empowered to live a righteous life to God's glory.

Like *Ruth* 1, chapter 2 involves a series of conversations. There are five dialogues: Ruth tells Naomi of her plan to go out to the fields (Ruth 2:2-3); Boaz greets his reapers and learns about Ruth (v 4-7); Boaz offers Ruth protection (v 8-15a); Boaz tells the reapers to help her (v 15b-16); and Ruth tells Naomi all that has happened (v 19-22). In terms of subject matter, three themes stand out all the way through: faith, favor, and hope. In this study, we will discuss the first three of these conversations, and understand the favor Boaz shows and the faith of both him and Ruth. In the following study we will move to the last two dialogues, seeing how hope rises for Ruth and Naomi, and how Boaz's favor points to the greater favor of God.

For behind it all is the hero of the story: the Lord. He is accomplishing his purposes. His providence is revealed beautifully in chapter 2. The Lord provides Boaz as the answer to Naomi's prayer, and the solution to the crisis of the family line.

OPTIONAL EXTRA
To help you imagine what happens in today's story, watch a video of people gleaning (collecting leftovers after a field has

been harvested). There are plenty of suitable videos online if you do a web search for "gleaning."

GUIDANCE FOR QUESTIONS

1. What do the phrases "a worthy man" or "a man of standing" make you think of?

• **Who would you apply this phrase to (either from history or someone alive today)?**
This question is designed to introduce a concept that comes up in Ruth 2:1 where Boaz is described as "a worthy man" (ESV) or "a man of standing" (NIV). You could come back to this later in the study to see how the people you name here compare with Boaz.

2. What do we learn about Boaz in verse 1?

• Boaz was a relative of Naomi's husband. He was "of the clan of Elimelech" (v 1). This phrase is significant. Later in the chapter, Naomi tells Ruth that Boaz "is one of our redeemers" (v 20; see also 3:9, 12). Boaz is a legal relative of Elimelech, which proves to be crucial in the narrative, due to Israelite laws and customs.

• Not only is Boaz a relative, but he is also a "worthy man" (Ruth 2:1). This phrase usually carries the idea of "war hero", however it can also mean "capable person" and "wealthy man." The story clearly shows Boaz to be a man of wealth and influence, having standing in the community (4:1-3, 9, 11). He does not fight battles, but he does own property and have servants. But there must be more than just wealth and influence in view: the same word is used to describe Ruth (3:11), who was poor. Boaz is not just a wealthy man; he is also a man with integrity and

godliness. In short, he is a man of both moral worth and material wealth.

• **What do verses 3, 4 and 11 add to this picture of Boaz?**

• Verse 3: Boaz owns at least one field of barley, near to Bethlehem.

• Verse 4: We are given a brief glimpse of Boaz's character by the way he greets his workers: "'The LORD be with you!' And they answered, 'The LORD bless you'" (v 4). Here is our first impression of Boaz—he greets his workers in the name of Yahweh. Boaz is saying, *Remember the presence and blessing of God in this field!* The workers respond to him with a similar greeting.

• Verse 11: Boaz has heard about Ruth (although he doesn't recognize her, v 5).

3. What does Ruth plan to do in verse 2? (See also Ruth 1:22.) The barley harvest is just beginning (1:22), so Ruth is planning to glean (collect leftovers) in the barley fields.

• **How does Naomi respond to Ruth's plan (v 2)?** Naomi gives Ruth permission to go and glean in the fields. We don't know how much Ruth understood about Old Testament laws for gleaning, but Naomi will have known that the law made provision for the poor, the widow, and the sojourner, and so Ruth was qualified to glean in the fields.

• **How hard does Ruth work (v 7; see also v 17)?** Ruth works very hard. She started in the "early morning" (v 7), with just a brief rest, and continued until the evening (v 17). When the foreman tells Boaz about Ruth, he emphasizes her impressive work ethic: she has had only a short rest all day. Here is another mark of Ruth's faith and humility: hard work. Faith in Yahweh does not mean being lazy and waiting around for him to act. Ruth tries to make the very best of her situation that she can, trusting God to be good to her as she does so.

4. Read Judges 21:25. How do Boaz and Ruth compare to most people in the days of the Judges? While most people were still doing "what was right in [their] own eyes" (Judges 21:25), Boaz was keeping God's rules about allowing the poor to glean in his fields (Leviticus 19:9-10). Ruth, likewise, chose to act according to the rules of gleaning, while working as hard as possible to provide for Naomi and herself. Remember that we are in the dark times of the judges: everyone was doing what was right in their own eyes, and we should not assume that the laws about gleaning were widely put into practice.

EXPLORE MORE
Read Deuteronomy 24:19-22 and Leviticus 19:9-10. What are the harvesters told to do and why? To leave behind any sheaves they forget, not beat the olive trees more than once, and not strip every grape from the vine (Deuteronomy 24:19, 20, 21). They are to leave the edges of the field for the poor, and not retrieve dropped crops (Leviticus 19:9-10). They are to do this in remembrance that they were once slaves in need (Deuteronomy 24:22).

Who is allowed to glean in the fields? The gleanings are left for "the sojourner, the fatherless, and the widow" (Deuteronomy 24:19,20,21) and "the poor" (Leviticus 19:10).

5. How does Boaz provide for Ruth (v 8-9)? Boaz decides to show favor to Ruth. After tenderly addressing Ruth as "my daughter" (v 8), Boaz authorizes her freedom to glean in his field, along with his own workers. Boaz does not only tell Ruth

that she may glean in his field, but insists that she stay there, telling her to "keep close to my young women" and "go after" them (v 9). He is determined to provide for her. He also shows her where to find water for refreshment. His word about drawing water is striking. Normally foreigners would draw water for Israelites, and women would draw it for men (Genesis 24:10-20). But she is given the freedom to drink from water already drawn by the Israelites. Boaz not only provides work and water for Ruth, but also protection. This is displayed by how he orders the men not to touch or harass Ruth. She is to be welcomed and protected, and not violated in any way.

• **Why (v 10-11)?** Ruth asks why Boaz is so kind to her (v 10). He explains that it's because of the kindness she in turn has shown to Naomi (v 11). Interestingly, when Boaz first sees Ruth in the field (v 5), he asks his foreman about this strange woman: "Whose young woman is this?". He wants to know something of her origins. He does not recognize her as the daughter-in-law of Naomi. In verses 11-12 it becomes clear that he had heard all about Ruth and what she has done for her mother-in-law, but in verse 5 he does not make the connection between the woman he has heard about and the woman he sees in his field. All he notices at this point is that she is out of place and by herself. It seems that he is concerned for her even before he knows about her situation and her character.

6. APPLY: Ruth is overwhelmed by the grace she receives from Boaz. How does her response in verse 10 point us to how we can respond to the grace God has shown us? When humility and grace meet, worship begins. We have received God's grace in an even greater way than

Ruth, as recipients of Jesus's saving grace (Ephesians 2:1-22). We should be even more overcome with gratitude, when we consider how the Savior has met our greatest need. We should fall on our knees often, asking, "Why have I found favor in your eyes, that you should take notice of me?"

- **Read Ephesians 2:8-9. As Christians, why have we "found favor" in God's eyes?** We have done nothing to earn or deserve God's favor. It's never based on our own works. It is purely "the gift of God" (v 8), and given because of Christ.

7. In addition to providing for Ruth, Boaz blesses her with his words. What does Boaz say to Ruth (v 11-12):

- **about her?** In verse 11, Boaz first speaks of Ruth's *reputation*. He had heard about Ruth's experience, how she had cared for Naomi, how she lost her husband, and how she had left her native land to join a new people. Word had spread about Ruth, and Boaz was impressed; so he expresses his admiration to her.

- **about God?** The Lord is a *refuge*. Boaz commends Ruth for abandoning the Moabite gods and taking "refuge" under the "wings" of the God of Israel. This image of finding refuge under the Lord's wings carries the idea of God's protection and his nurturing care for his people.

- **about what he's praying?** In verse 12, Boaz continues to encourage Ruth by *praying* that God will reward her faith. Boaz believes that what Ruth has done is a result of her faith in God. It is the Lord whom she has pleased by her actions.

8. How does this make Ruth feel (v 13)?

In response to Boaz's kindness, Ruth expresses her gratitude. She expresses relief, humility, and a deep sense of thankfulness.

She recognizes that she is not even one of Boaz's "servants", and yet he has blessed her in word and deed. Her race and her class did not prevent Boaz from showing her compassion. Ruth had had no idea what the day would bring, but by God's grace she found herself in a field of favor. You can imagine what the affirmation of a godly, influential leader must have sounded like to Ruth. His encouragement surely lifted her spirits and gave her a sense of dignity.

9. How do we see Boaz living out this verse (Micah 6:8) in Ruth 2:1-13?

- First, Boaz *provides for the hungry*. He does justice by following the Lord's word regarding the widow, the stranger, and the poor, allowing Ruth gleaning rights. Many landowners were not friendly to this law. And it is easy to imagine how some may have justified to themselves not providing for the poor, as they recovered from a ten-year famine! Yet Boaz obeyed the word to "do justice."

- Second, Boaz not only provides for Ruth, but he also *protects her*. He serves as Ruth's justice advocate, charging the men not to harm her. Boaz thus reflects Proverbs 31:8-9, which tells us that "judg[ing] righteously" means "defend[ing] the rights of the poor and needy." He uses his influence for those who have no influence.

- Third, Boaz *uses his words to bless Ruth*, showing her personal dignity and respect. He goes *beyond* the requirements of the law—he showers this desperate foreigner with grace. He offers Ruth refreshment (v 9); he honors her faith (v 11); he prays for her (v 12); and he speaks kindly to her (v 13). In the following verses, he even invites her to his table for food and fellowship (v 14). Finally, he urges the men to allow her to glean more than she ever imagined (v 15-16). This is more than justice: Boaz shows that he "love[s] kindness."

- Fourth, Boaz *shows kindness and grace not only to Ruth, but also to his workers.* His greeting to his workers in the field, and their response, indicates that his workers respect him.
- Fifth, Boaz *walks humbly with the Lord.* This is evidenced in many ways. His consideration of Ruth, his way of addressing his workers, his acknowledgement of the Lord's sovereignty, and as we shall see, his willingness to eat with his workers, are expressions of a humble walk before the Lord. No wonder he and Ruth make such

a good match! Humility is displayed in them both.

10. APPLY: What would someone in your church family who lived out Micah 6:8 be doing with their time and money? What will it look like in your particular church or group, in the specific neighborhood God has placed you in, to "do justice", "love kindness", and "walk humbly with your God"? Some answers to this question may be things you are already doing, in which case thank God for them. See if you can also think of something new, that you are not doing, that can enable you to live out Micah 6:8 in your community.

Ruth 2:14-23

4 HOSPITALITY, KINDNESS, AND HOPE

THE BIG IDEA

Boaz is a redeemer who shows hospitality and generosity, and who gives Ruth and Naomi hope. He points forward to Christ as our Redeemer.

SUMMARY

The first half of *Ruth* 2 showed us the character of Boaz, a man of both moral worth and material wealth. In the latter half, we also learn that Boaz is a "redeemer" (v 20).

Boaz's favor extends to the dinner table (v 14). The narrator describes Boaz's welcome and provision. Boaz meets Ruth's need and more. The writer says, "she was

satisfied, and she had some left over." Leftovers! With whom is she going to share these? Naomi, of course (v 18)!

After the meal, Ruth prepares to continue gleaning. Again, Boaz goes beyond the letter of the law. He charges the workers not to insult or mistreat Ruth. He also gives Ruth the special privilege of gleaning "among the sheaves" (v 15; that is, "the grain among the bundles," CSB). Normally gleaning meant picking up grain that had been discarded or left behind accidentally by the harvesters, but here Ruth is invited to take the pick of the crop—the grain that has already been harvested. Boaz even tells the workers to pull some of the stalks from the bundles and leave them for Ruth to gather (v 16).

As a result, Ruth gathers an abundance: a whole "ephah of barley" (v 17). She brings home some 30 pounds (13.6 kg) of food! That would be several weeks' worth of food.

Ruth had left Naomi's searching for favor. She found it in Boaz. Now she returns to Naomi with leftovers and a load of barley (v 18). A conversation about her day and about Boaz ensues.

Naomi tells Ruth: "The man is a close relative of ours, one of our redeemers" (v 20). Naomi's mind must have been racing at this point! The Hebrew word *go'el* ("redeemer") is significant. It means a "kinsman-redeemer," a close relative who is able to come to the aid of a family member. This concept is introduced here and will be developed in chapter 3.

In one sense, Boaz has already acted as a *go'el* by providing for Ruth and Naomi. But Naomi has more in mind, because she knows what God's law says about the role of a redeemer.

The chapter concludes with Ruth staying close to Boaz's young women, gleaning until the end of the barley and wheat harvests, and continuing to live with her mother-in-law (v 23).

Since we have just now been introduced to Boaz as a "redeemer," a consideration of this biblical mega-theme is fitting at this point. We need to consider four aspects of redemption in *Ruth* and across the biblical storyline: (1) the need for redemption, (2) the price of redemption, (3) the nature of the redeemer, and (4) the familial nature of redemption.

We need redemption because we are weak and helpless. All examples of redemption in the Bible include this element. In *Ruth*, the need is about food and family. They need provision now, and they need security for the future. They cannot solve this on their own: they need a redeemer. A husband and a child for Ruth will solve the crisis, provide for their needs, and continue their family line.

When we look *at* Boaz, we see many godly traits to imitate. But when we look *through* Boaz, we see the gospel of Jesus Christ. Jesus sees us in our need, pays the price for our redemption, gives us a new status, and brings us into the most intimate of relationships. How do we respond to such grace? Ruth's response to Boaz (v 10) points in the right direction: to fall before our Redeemer and worship the one who has shown us *hesed*.

OPTIONAL EXTRA

Today's passage takes place at a mealtime. Ask the group how many versions of saying/singing grace they know. If your study starts with a meal, or even just coffee, thank God for it by saying grace together.

GUIDANCE FOR QUESTIONS

1. When were you last invited to join someone for a meal? How did they show you that you were welcome?
• **Have you ever been to a meal where you weren't made welcome? What was that like? How did you feel?**
In today's passage, Boaz invites Ruth to join him and his workers for a midday meal. He makes her very welcome and gives her more than she needs to eat.

2. Think back to the previous study. What did you discover about Boaz's character? (If group members need to refresh their memories, they can look back at questions 2, 4 and 5 of the previous study.) Ruth 2:1 says that Boaz is "a worthy man" (ESV) or "a man of standing (NIV). He greets his workers in the name of the Lord (v 4). He keeps God's rules about allowing the poor to glean in his fields (v 3, 8-9). He is kind and generous to Ruth (v 8-9). Boaz is unlike most people of his time, who "did what was right in [their] own eyes" (Judges 21:25).

- **What does Boaz do in verses 14-16 that match what you already know about him?** Verse 14: Boaz is generous to Ruth, welcoming her to the midday meal and giving her more than she can eat. Verses 15-16: Boaz went above and beyond the laws of gleaning by instructing his workers to let Ruth glean among the sheaves and to pull out extra barley for her.

- **What is the result for Ruth (v 17-18)?** Verse 17: Ruth kept gleaning until the evening, when she then "beat out what she had gleaned." The result was a huge amount—an ephah of barley (enough food for several weeks). Verse 18: Ruth also had food left over from her midday meal that she was able to give to Naomi.

3 Naomi had a lot to say when Ruth came home (v 19-22). What questions did Naomi ask? Verse 19: "Where did you glean today?" and "Where have you worked?" Naomi knew that Ruth had gone to glean in the fields (2:2), but not which field she ended up in or who owned it.

- **What did Naomi then say about Boaz?** Verse 19: "Blessed be the man who took notice of you." Verse 20: "May he be blessed by the LORD, whose kindness has not forsaken the living or the dead!" and "The man is a close relative of ours, one of our redeemers." Verse 22: "It is good, my daughter, that

you go out with [Boaz's] young women, lest in another field you be assaulted."

4. Do you find the end of chapter 2 encouraging or discouraging, and why?
- It's *encouraging* that Ruth has somewhere safe to work until the end of the barley and wheat harvests (v 21), and that this means she and Naomi have plenty of food to eat. It's even more encouraging that Naomi sees that God's kindness is at the center of Boaz's kindness (v 20).
- But it's potentially *discouraging* that the harvests have finished by the end of verse 23, leaving Ruth and Naomi facing the same problems as before. They have no income to pay for food and necessities, and no husband for Ruth. The romantic reader may see the chapter ending on a downer. After the completion of the harvests, nothing is said of the potential relationship between Boaz and Ruth—nor any other plan for future provision. Ruth would have been in regular contact with Boaz for these six to seven weeks, yet nothing is said of their relationship developing. Now the harvest season is over, and Ruth is still living with her mother-in-law. She is still a widow at the end of chapter 2. We must wait for the next chapter to see how things progress between her and Boaz.

5. Verse 14 shows us Boaz's hospitality at the mealtime. What do we learn about Boaz from this scene?
- First, his style of leadership. Even though he is a wealthy boss, he still eats with his workers. He associates with them—as Paul instructs Christians to do in Romans 12:16b.
- Second, he not only eats alongside the workers, but he also acts as the host of the meal. He urges Ruth to eat of what

has been provided and also serves her the roasted grain personally. This says something about his attitude. He serves. He leads with grace. His attitude is one of humility and warmth—important traits in a leader.

- Third, he provides more than enough. He is not a stingy leader. The scene is a picture of abundance.
- Fourth, Boaz not only grants Ruth the freedom to glean, but he welcomes her into his group of workers. He gives her a seat next to the reapers, which provides a sense of honor and dignity.

In all this, Boaz goes well beyond the requirements of the law, lavishing his grace upon Ruth. He exemplifies hesed—the same loving kindness that God shows to his people.

PRAY

Now would be a great moment to pray. It is hard for many of us to adequately appreciate having enough food to satisfy our needs. But to a poor, desperate widow, this meal would have been wonderful. We should pause, thank God for our daily bread, and ask him to use us to bless those who are in need—not only materially, but also relationally with an attitude of warmth.

6. APPLY: Meals with others are about more than food. How can you apply Boaz's example to meals with your church family, with your neighbors, and with your own family? Boaz associated with his workers, acted as host, provided more than enough, and welcomed Ruth into his group of workers. Encourage your group members to think about how they can display some of these same qualities. For example, how can they make sure they associate with a range of people at a church family meal?

7. NEED: Fill in the table below to show some of the reasons why the New Testament says we need to be redeemed. See table at the bottom of the page.

- **It has been said that, to become a Christian, "all you need is need." What do you think this means?** The great tragedy today is that many do not see their need for salvation. It is easy for people to see Ruth's need for a husband, but many are blind to their own need for spiritual redemption. It is only when we recognise our need—and that we are helpless and hopeless in our sin—that we will come to Christ to redeem us.

Passage	Why we are helpless	What we need
Romans 6:17-18	Slaves to sin	To be set free from sin / slaves of righteousness
Ephesians 2:12-13	Alienated from God	To be brought near by the blood of Christ
Colossians 1:13-14	In the kingdom of darkness	To be transferred to the Son's kingdom of light
John 10:11	Lost sheep	To be rescued by the Good Shepherd

8. *PRICE:* **We will see the price of redeeming Ruth and Naomi in Ruth 3 – 4. What does the New Testament say about the price of redeeming us in 1 Corinthians 6:20 and 1 Peter 1:18-19?** We were "bought with a price" (1 Corinthians 6:20). That price was "the precious blood of Christ" (1 Peter 1:19).

9. *NATURE:* **To be a redeemer you have to have both the willingness and the ability to redeem. As we will see, Boaz had both. How does Philippians 2:6-8 show Jesus' willingness to redeem?** Jesus willingly "made himself nothing" (v 7, NIV) and "humbled himself" (v 8).

• **How does Jesus' ability to redeem exceed that of Boaz (see Revelation 5:9)?** Boaz redeemed two women. Christ came to redeem not just one person but people "from every tribe and language and people and nation."

10. *FAMILY:* **Read Galatians 4:4-7. What familial image is used to describe what it is like to be redeemed by Christ?** The redeemed are the "adopted": Christians become the children of God, brothers and sisters in God's household. Adoption is free for the one who is adopted, but costly for the one who adopts. It cost Jesus his life and death. He lived the life we could never have lived—keeping God's law perfectly—and died the death we should have died.

EXPLORE MORE
Look up some other examples where redemption is linked with loving or familial language:
• **Deuteronomy 7:6-8:** God chose the Israelites to be his people, his "treasured possession" (v 6). He redeemed them (from slavery in Egypt) because he loved them (v 8).

• **Isaiah 54:5:** Isaiah describes God as "Maker," "husband," and "Redeemer."
• **Isaiah 63:16:** Here Isaiah describes God as both "Father" and "redeemer."

11. APPLY: Think of one or more non-Christians you want to share the gospel with. At this moment, do they most need to understand their need of redemption, the price it cost, the nature of Jesus the Redeemer, or the family they would be redeemed into? Encourage each member of your group to think of at least one person they'd like to share the gospel with. Encourage everyone to write an answer down as this makes it more likely that they will remember and act upon what they've written.

5 Ruth 3:1-18
COLD FEET

THE BIG IDEA

Naomi devises a *plan* (3:1-5); it will lead to Ruth's *proposal* to Boaz (v 6-9); Boaz will respond with a *promise* to Ruth (v 10-13), and by *providing* for her (v 14-18).

SUMMARY

"A good man is hard to find." It is true today, and it was true in the days of Ruth.

In *Ruth* 2, we met a good man—Boaz. He was described as a "worthy man" (2:1), a man of substance (both materially and morally). He was single, a potential redeemer, and a man of mercy and justice. He lavished kindness on Ruth and her mother-in-law, and Naomi recognized that he could be a redeemer for them, marrying Ruth. But chapter 2 leaves us hanging! We are left to wonder: will anything happen between these two?

The story begins with the rejuvenated Naomi expressing her desire to find Ruth a husband. Instead of being self-absorbed, Naomi is now looking out for Ruth's welfare, a sign that God's *hesed* is melting Naomi's cold heart.

She reminds Ruth that Boaz is a relative (v 2) and informs her that he will be "winnowing barley tonight" at the threshing floor (the place where farmers would separate grain from chaff).

Naomi provides specific instructions for Ruth (3:3-4). We do not read of this specific method anywhere else in Scripture—and there are aspects of this plan that we would not recommend to our daughters! But the riskiness of the strategy she commends to Ruth serves to expose the one thing that

will make it secure: Boaz. If Naomi has over-estimated his kindness, integrity, and status as a close family member, the plan will go seriously wrong. The plan all and only depends upon Boaz.

The same is true for us as Christian believers. As we make plans, we know that there is one person on whom everything depends: the Lord Jesus.

The plan has been hatched; and now Ruth goes to the threshing floor, "just as her mother-in-law had commanded her" (v 6). She waits until Boaz's heart was "merry," having finished his meal. She observes where he lays down, and then she quietly enters: "she came softly and uncovered his feet and lay down" (v 7). We can feel the tension as Boaz feels the air on his feet…

Stepping back for a moment, we are left to marvel at the purity of both Boaz and Ruth. Instead of engaging in some steamy sexual encounter, Boaz praises Yahweh for Ruth! Nor does Ruth make any sexual advances to Boaz in an effort to win him.

In the morning, before he approaches the other redeemer at the city gate, Boaz extends grace once again to Ruth and Naomi. Before it is light enough for people to recognize Ruth, Boaz sends her home (v 14). This early send-off is meant to preserve her dignity and reputation—things that obviously matter to Boaz.

He sends Ruth off with a gift. Telling her to hold out her garment, he proceeds to put six measures of barley on it (v 15). It is such a large amount that Boaz has to "put it on her," either on her head, on her back, or over her back: an amount that was most likely around 60-90 lb (30-40 kg) of grain. She then carried it all the way home!

This generous provision of food seems to have been provided for at least three reasons. First, it was a means of basic provision for two desperate widows. Second, it would have explained why Ruth had been at Boaz's threshing floor, should anyone see her leaving. Third, and most significantly, it was a symbolic provision—a message to Naomi.

This same Naomi once described herself as "empty" (1:21). Then, she was both childless and hungry; now, she has a full load of grain before her. We are witnessing Naomi's journey from emptiness to fullness, through the actions of Ruth and Boaz. Her days of emptiness are soon to be over.

OPTIONAL EXTRA

Find something that weighs at least 20kg. Try lifting it above your head. The amount of barley Boaz gives to Ruth in chapter 3 probably weighed twice as much as this (60-90 lb or 30-40 kg). It was a very generous gift!

GUIDANCE FOR QUESTIONS

1. If you're married, who proposed and how? Do you know any stories about unusual marriage proposals? In today's passage there is a very unusual marriage proposal between Ruth and Boaz. When you reach it, you may want to remind the group of their answers to this opening question.

2. Who initiated Ruth's meeting with Boaz? It was *Naomi's* plan, which then involved Ruth initiating a meeting with Boaz. Once again, we see that even though the book of Ruth highlights the providence of God, the characters do not slip into passive fatalism. They are active, not disengaged.

3. Naomi could have said "God is sovereign, so let's just wait until a husband knocks on the door." Why do you think she didn't do that? God's sovereignty is not a licence for human inactivity. That would not be trusting the Lord but testing the Lord. No, we should work and act, in view of and because of God's work and God's activity.

4. Naomi provides specific instructions for Ruth (v 3-4). What are the seven steps she proposes?

1. Wash... yourself / take a bath (v 3). This is always good advice when pursuing a spouse!

2. Put on... some perfume (v 3). Scented oils were common in this time and helpful given the fact that modern deodorants didn't exist.

3. Put on... some fresh clothes (v 3). Ruth must no longer look like a widow in mourning.

4. Visit... Boaz at the threshing floor when he is in a good mood (v 3). After a hard day's work, some good food, and a sip of wine, Boaz will be relaxed. Sure enough, in verse 7, we are told that "his heart was merry."

5. Observe... where Boaz lies down (v 4). Ruth definitely needs to follow this step: make sure it is Boaz!

6. Uncover... Boaz's feet and lie down close to him (v 4). We can sense the tension in these instructions. The purpose of such a sensual gesture is to communicate something to Boaz. Apparently, this nonverbal gesture was a customary means of requesting marriage, something that Ruth will eventually communicate verbally.

7. Listen... to Boaz's instructions (v 4).

Naomi trustingly leaves the matter to Boaz. She has made her plans, but the Lord will determine the next steps (Proverbs 16:9).

5. How does Ruth respond to Naomi's plan (v 5)? In verse 5, we read of Ruth's remarkable commitment to the plan: "All that you say I will do." We see Ruth's loyalty to Naomi here, as well as her courage. Both Ruth and Naomi are showing tremendous trust in Boaz's integrity.

6. APPLY: This risky strategy depends on the kindness, the integrity, and the status as a kinsman-redeemer, of Boaz. For us, too, there is one person on whom everything depends: the Lord Jesus.

- **How is Jesus the "perfect Boaz"?** Jesus is a Redeemer and Bridegroom of perfect kindness and integrity.

- **What risks can Christians take because of the kindness, integrity, and redeeming power of Jesus?** The risks we take, to live for Jesus and to further his kingdom, will depend on the extent that we know we can trust him. When we hold back and play safe, we are often betraying a small view of Jesus: a suspicion deep down that he may not come through for us, that he cannot be trusted to do what is best for us. When we see him as he is—the perfect Boaz—then we can joyfully lean on his character, living in such a way that only makes sense because he is who he is.

7. Does Ruth follow Naomi's plan exactly? Compare verse 4 with verse 9. No, Ruth does not follow Naomi's plan exactly. Instead of waiting on Boaz's instructions, Ruth takes the initiative. She is essentially proposing to Boaz when she says, "Spread your wings over your servant, for you are a redeemer" (v 9). She

communicates her desires to him. She is not interested in some dirty one-night stand. She is interested in marriage—the idiom "spread your wings" elsewhere is an idiom for marriage (see Ezekiel 16:8). Boaz also used this expression previously to describe how Ruth sought refuge under the wings of Yahweh (Ruth 2:12). Now Ruth is asking Boaz to become part of God's protection and provision for her life.

- **How does Boaz respond to Ruth's request (v 10-11)?**
  - Before giving Ruth a direct answer to her proposal, Boaz blesses Ruth (v 10).
  - Boaz was impressed before (2:11) by Ruth's kindness toward Naomi in choosing to journey to Bethlehem with her. Now the "kindness" (*hesed*) referred to is Ruth's desire to provide Naomi with an heir by marrying Boaz.
  - Added to this is Boaz's delight that Ruth has not "gone after other young men, whether poor or rich" (3:10). Based upon this statement, it seems safe to assume Ruth is younger than Boaz, and it also seems that Ruth is more attractive than Boaz. She could have gone after young men (or, literally, "choice men"), but she has decided not to pursue a guy out of greed (the "rich"), nor out of attraction and passion (the "poor")— this is a hint that she was capable of attaining either because of her own youthful attractiveness. Instead Ruth has other values, such as family loyalty.
  - In verse 11, Boaz comforts Ruth by saying, "do not fear." We can imagine how fast Ruth's heart must have been beating—this is the crucial moment of decision. And Boaz promises to do everything that she has requested, which probably includes taking care of the family and property, not just marrying Ruth.

- **How does this relate to what we already know of Boaz's character?** Ruth already knows something of the character of Boaz (and so do we): he is willing to follow the spirit of the law, not just the minimum expectations of it. Ruth experienced his kindness when she went to glean in his fields (2:8-16).

- **What is the possible hitch in the plan (v 12)?** Just as the happy ending seems secured, Boaz raises a problem: there is an unnamed man who is a closer relative than him (v 12). The happy ending is put on hold. The other relative has a more legitimate claim than Boaz, and Boaz honors this social custom. But Boaz pledges under God that if the other man is unwilling to redeem her, he himself will marry her. Either way, Ruth will have a redeemer. Boaz then urges Ruth to remain with him during the night for the purpose of safety (nothing in the text indicates any kind of sinful activity overnight). Ruth will not have to approach this other relative directly, for Boaz will address him personally the next day.

8. Read Deuteronomy 25:5-10. If a married man died without having a son to carry on the family name, what was his brother obligated to do? The dead man's brother (the kinsman-redeemer) was obligated to marry his brother's widow in order to raise up for the dead brother a family who could inherit his property.

- **If he refused, how was his brother's widow able to get justice (v 7)?** The widow could bring her case to the elders who met at the town gate. They would instruct the man to keep the law. If he refused, his own name would be tarnished (v 9-10).

- **Does this ruling about the duties of a kinsman-redeemer apply to Boaz?** Boaz is "a redeemer" but not *the only* redeemer: he is not the closest family member. Nor was Boaz the brother of Elimelech, nor of his sons. Remember, under certain circumstances, the kinsman-redeemer was obligated to marry his *brother's* widow, but Boaz was not in this precise position. He did have a family connection with Naomi and Ruth, so it was possible for him to act in the spirit of the law and become a redeemer. But we must not think that Boaz had no choice in this matter. He was not the brother. Otherwise, this whole midnight drama would be unnecessary. Ruth could just go up and ask him to marry her in the daylight, appealing to the law.

EXPLORE MORE
Read Proverbs 31:10-31
The book of Ruth allows us to see an example of what a Proverbs 31 woman looks like in an ungodly culture. What similarities can you see? Proverbs 31 is an alphabetic acrostic of 22 lines, celebrating a worthy woman. The similarities between Proverbs 31 and Ruth are noticeable. In their book *Unceasing Kindness* (p 42), Peter Lau and Gregory Goswell note the following:

- Both women are energetic and active (Proverbs 31:15, 27; Ruth 2:2, 7, 17).
- Both work to supply the needs of their households (Proverbs 31:15, 21; Ruth 2:18).
- Both show kindness (*hesed*; Proverbs 31:26; Ruth 3:10).
- Both are praised as superior by their husbands and by others (Proverbs 31:28-29; Ruth 3:10-11; 4:15).
- Both work hard (Proverbs 31:13, 27; Ruth 2:2, 17, 23).
- Both fear God (Proverbs 31:30; Ruth 1:16; 2:12).

Boaz also notes that all his fellow townsmen recognize Ruth as a "worthy woman," (Ruth 3:11) a phrase which also occurs in Proverbs 31:10. They esteem Ruth—as Proverbs 31:31 puts it, "her works praise her in the gates." Ruth is a Proverbs 31 lady, who is respected and praised by others. Her ultimate beauty is her godliness.

9. Ruth returns to Naomi with six measures of barley (60-90 pounds or 30-40 kg of grain). What extra information does Ruth tell her mother-in-law, and how does Naomi respond (Ruth 3:17-18)? Ruth includes something that the narrator did not previously include (v 17). Boaz's gift was intended to bless *Naomi*. Boaz is serious about his pursuit of Ruth—so serious that this will involve caring for her mother-in-law, too. To symbolize this, he provides this extravagant gift.

Naomi recognizes Boaz's serious commitment to meet with their closer relative. She tells Ruth to wait "until you learn how the matter turns out, for the man will not rest but will settle [accomplish, finish] the matter today" (v 18). Naomi trusts Boaz to resolve the complication immediately, and so she urges Ruth to wait until he does just that.

10. APPLY: Sometimes, when we read a Bible story, it gives us a direct example to follow. But Ruth 3 contains much that we cannot imitate, such as threshing-floor marriage proposals! Think again about the actions of Naomi, Ruth and Boaz in this chapter. How can you apply their example to your own lives this week? Encourage each group member to think of at least one application they can make from this passage.

Ruth 4:1-12

6 TAKE MY SANDAL

THE BIG IDEA
Redeeming Ruth is not straightforward: there is a price to pay. The question is: which man will pay it?

SUMMARY
Boaz is seeking to resolve the matter of there being a closer relative who may choose to marry Ruth. Understanding this legal transaction will help us to see how wonderful Boaz' redemption of Ruth is.

Boaz goes up to the city gate and sits down (Ruth 4:1). Legal transactions, judicial proceedings, and official business were all conducted at the city gate (Genesis 23:18; 34:20, 24; 2 Samuel 15:2-6; Proverbs 22:22; Amos 5:12, 15). It was a spacious place for people to assemble, like a modern-day courthouse. Further, it was also the best place to find someone. Everyone in the city regularly passed through this gate. So Boaz sits here to wait.

"And behold, the redeemer, of whom Boaz had spoken, came by" (Ruth 4:1). Again, the word "behold" is used to heighten the tension.

Boaz asks this man to sit with him. Once he is seated, Boaz asks the ruling body (ten of the town's elders) to sit down as well (v 2).

Boaz then explains the matter to the anonymous redeemer. But Boaz does not begin with Ruth, but with Naomi, and a piece of property belonging to Elimelech. It is this "parcel of land" that he tells the other redeemer he has the right to buy.

The anonymous redeemer responds earnestly to the proposal. This was a good deal. But the deal is not yet final. Boaz has something else to say. "The day you buy the field from the hand of Naomi, you also acquire Ruth the Moabite" (v 5).

The narrator does not explain all the details of the laws here. The point is that we notice the interests and attitudes of the two potential redeemers.

A true redeemer is the kind of person who is willing to pay a price for the good of others, and that is a mark of Boaz, not the other relative. It is fitting that no one knows this man's name, while Boaz, who reflects the selfless love of Christ (Philippians 2:1-11), is remembered as a member of the line of the Messiah.

Boaz is willing to pay the price necessary to marry Ruth, and the closer relative is not—and so Boaz's "purchase" is confirmed through an ancient custom: "When the redeemer said to Boaz, 'Buy it for yourself,' he drew off his sandal" (Ruth 4:8).

Then one more significant thing happens at the city gate: a three-fold prayer of blessing from the people and the elders.

The narrator does not tell us how the news got back to Ruth and Naomi. All we are told next is that Boaz took Ruth as his wife (Ruth 4:13).

One thing is for certain: Boaz was unique. To be a redeemer, one needed to be a relative and to have the willingness to redeem. The nearer relative was not willing

to pay the price, but Boaz was.

The reluctance of the other relative to marry Ruth, and his concern about his own inheritance, highlights the amazing commitment and selflessness of Boaz, who laid down his own interests to redeem Ruth. The narrator shows us the legal implications of redemption in order that we may see the love that motivates it.

Boaz was special, but our Redeemer, Jesus Christ, is even more special. Boaz may have impaired his inheritance to redeem Ruth, but Jesus was actually willing to empty himself and go to the cross to secure our redemption.

OPTIONAL EXTRA

Look online for pictures of the "Bethlehem City Gate" or "Old Testament city gates", or look up Ruth in an illustrated children's Bible, to get a feel for how the gate in today's passage may have looked.

GUIDANCE FOR QUESTIONS

1. What procedures have you needed to follow to make any legal transactions or agreements (such as buying a house or car, or getting married)? There is a legal transaction in today's reading that will seem strange to many of us. It involves taking off a sandal.

2. Verses 1-12 all happen at the city gate. Imagine that you are filming these verses for television. How might you break the events up into a series of different scenes? This question is designed to give a feel for the order in which things happened at the city gate, and the moments of tension. There's no one "right" answer. One possible way to film this would be as follows:
a. Boaz goes to the city gate and then sits

down to wait.

b. The other possible redeemer walks past, is spotted by Boaz, and is invited to come and sit with Boaz and ten of the town elders.

c. Boaz tells the other redeemer about the sale of Naomi's land. "I will redeem it," says the other redeemer.

d. Boaz then drops the bombshell that buying Naomi's land would also mean marrying her daughter-in-law, Ruth. "I cannot redeem it," says the other redeemer.

e. The other redeemer takes his sandal off and gives it to Boaz.

f. Boaz informs the town elders, and everyone else at the city gate, that he will buy Naomi's land and marry Ruth.

g. "You are witnesses," says Boaz. "We are witnesses," say the people.

3. Compare Ruth 2:4, 3:8 and 4:1. How does the author of *Ruth* use "and behold" within this book? The phrase "and behold" heightens tension within the narrative. It also shows us that the unseen hand of God is at work. It was the Lord who brought Boaz to his field on the first day Ruth went there to glean (2:4); and it was the Lord who brought the other potential redeemer to the city gate while Boaz was there waiting for him (4:1).

4. How does the other redeemer respond to Boaz's initial suggestion (v 4)? What changes in verse 6 and why? Initially, the other redeemer is happy to buy Naomi's land (v 4); but when he learns that it will also mean marrying Ruth, he changes his mind (v 6). He does not want to lose any of his own land and inheritance, which he would do if he followed the law of redemption (that Ruth's son would be considered as Mahlon's son).

• **This other redeemer is never named in the narrative. Why do you think that might be?** His anonymity in the narrative may simply reflect the fact that he will be dismissed in the story and forgotten. But there could be more. Perhaps he is left anonymous to save his family from embarrassment. Or the narrator might also be implying that this man is not worth naming, due to his self-centeredness and his failure to act on behalf of his relatives (v 5).

5. APPLY: When the other redeemer was given the option of buying land that would bring profit to him and his family, he was keen to do so. But he changed his mind when he heard about marrying Ruth, saying "I cannot redeem it for myself, lest I impair my own inheritance" (v 6). Can you think of examples from your church family where someone has acted in a godly way even though it has cost them financially or personally to do so? For example, someone not going away for a holiday so that the money they save can be given to gospel work, or someone giving their car to a missionary. Many Christians choose to keep their giving secret, so be careful not to break any confidences.

6. How did the other redeemer confirm the transaction with Boaz, and who witnessed it? As was the custom at the time, he took off his sandal and gave it to Boaz (v 7-8). This was witnessed by the town elders and the other people who were at the city gate (v 9, 11).

• **What did Boaz redeem on that day?** The land that belonged to Elimelech (v 3, 5), everything else that belonged to Elimelech or his sons Chilion and Mahlon (v 9), and Ruth to be his wife (v 10).

7. Compare the other redeemer with Boaz. What do they have in common? How are they different?

- In common: They are both relatives of Elimelech, Naomi's late husband. So both of them qualify as possible kinsman-redeemers for Naomi, though Boaz is not as close a relative as the other redeemer. They both live in Bethlehem. They both follow the customs for agreeing legal transactions.

- Different: The other redeemer initially says he will redeem Naomi's land, but then changes his mind when he hears he will have to marry Ruth. Boaz has already told Ruth that he will redeem her if he can (Ruth 3:11-13), and he keeps his word to her (4:10).

- **What do you think the priorities are for each man?**

  - Verse 6 makes it clear that the other redeemer is focused on himself. He is unwilling to do anything that might "impair [his] own inheritance." He is more concerned with his own welfare, property, and posterity than with the welfare of his relative, Naomi.

  - In contrast, we have already seen the good character of Boaz in the previous chapters. He is a godly man who not only intends to act as a true redeemer according to Old Testament law but also to keep the promises he has made to Ruth and Naomi.

8. A true redeemer is willing to pay a price for the good of others. How is this true of Boaz? How is Jesus Christ the ultimate Kinsman-Redeemer?

- To be sure, it would cost Boaz money to redeem the property; but acquiring Ruth as well would require resolve and even the risk of losing a good reputation (since, as Boaz emphasizes, Ruth was a Moabite).

- Boaz was special, but our Redeemer, Jesus Christ, is even more special. Boaz may have impaired his inheritance to redeem Ruth, but Jesus was actually willing to empty himself and go to the cross to secure our redemption. In his great love, he laid down his life for his bride. He redeemed us because he loved us (Ephesians 5:25). The story of Ruth gives us a concrete example of the romance of redemption and points us to this even greater union, of which every Christian, single or married, is a part and a beneficiary.

EXPLORE MORE
Read Philippians 2:1-11. How do verses 6-11 show Jesus acting as our Kinsman-Redeemer? How do verses 1-5 match the character and actions of Boaz?
Verses 6-11: Jesus "made himself nothing, taking the form of a servant, being born in the likeness of men" (v 7). As a human, he was now our Kinsman. He "humbled himself by becoming obedient to the point of death, even death on a cross" (v 9). This is how Jesus "redeemed" us.
Verses 1-5: Boaz shows the "same mind" and "same love" (v 2) as Jesus. He "look[ed] not only to his own interests, but also to the interests of others" (v 4) in caring for Ruth and Naomi, even at a cost to himself.

9. One more significant thing happens at the city gate: a three-fold prayer of blessing from the people and the elders. What are the three blessings (Ruth 4:11-12)?

- The first blessing is directed to Ruth: "May the LORD make the woman, who is coming into your house, like Rachel and Leah, who together built up the house of Israel" (v 11a). Rachel and Leah were the wives of Jacob: with their two handmaidens, Bilhah and Zilpah, they bore him twelve sons, whose descendants made up the twelve tribes of Israel (Genesis 29-30; 35:16-18). The Lord is the one who enabled both Leah and Rachel to have children: in each case he "opened her womb" (29:31; 30:22). Leah was the mother of Judah (25:23), the ancestor of the tribe of Naomi and Boaz. The people, then, are asking the Lord to give Ruth a place alongside these mothers of the people of God: that is, that she may be given a key role among God's people.

- The second prayer of blessing is pointed toward Boaz: "May you act worthily in Ephrathah and be renowned in Bethlehem" (Ruth 4:11b). This is not just a prayer for prosperity and a good reputation: it is a prayer for righteousness. Boaz's renown will come from his worthy actions—the kindness, compassion, and integrity that we have seen in the book of *Ruth*.

- The final blessing is directed to the family as a whole: "and may your house be like the house of Perez, whom Tamar bore to Judah" (v 12). Tamar was the widow of Judah's son (Genesis 38:6-7). She too had lost her husband and was childless. As with Ruth, Tamar's family line was threatened and it seemed that her husband's name would die out. Tamar had no prospect of marrying again: her father-in-law, Judah, had promised that she would marry another of his sons, as the law demanded, but he had not kept his promise (v 11, 14). So Tamar disguised herself as a prostitute, deceiving her own father-in-law, so that she might have a child by him (v 15-16).

- NOTE: If your group have further questions about Tamar, explain some or all of the following: Both Ruth and Tamar went out in active pursuit of a child and a better

future. Of course, Ruth revealed her identity and received a child legitimately through marriage, whereas Tamar concealed her identity and deceived Judah. Moreover, Boaz's behavior toward Ruth was only ever godly, whereas Judah's conduct was precisely the opposite. Both unions, however, in the providence of God, proved to play an important role in salvation history. God promised that the Messiah would come through Judah (Genesis 49:10), and his strongest son was Perez: of all the sons of Judah, it is Perez' descendants whose line is followed in the tribal genealogy of 1 Chronicles 2:3 – 3:24.

- **How were these prayers answered?** Ruth did become a key person in the story of redemptive history. Boaz's family did have renown in Bethlehem. And it was through Boaz that Israel's king would come. At this point, the people of Israel have not even asked for a king (though they do need one—Judges 21:25), but from this man Boaz, King David would emerge.

10. APPLY: How has this study helped your appreciation of the character and love of Jesus your Redeemer to grow? What aspect of Jesus' character do you most want to hold on to this week? Encourage each member of your group to give at least one answer to this question, and to think about how this will make a difference to them in the coming week.

7 Ruth 4:13-22
THE PROMISED SON

THE BIG IDEA

At the end of the book of *Ruth*, the narrator shows us four ways that God was at work in the lives of Naomi, Ruth, and Boaz: God provides a son for Boaz and Ruth, a redeemer for Naomi, a king for Israel, and the Messiah for the world..

SUMMARY

In this closing section of *Ruth*, the narrator ties up some of the dominant ideas in the book, showing how God has not forgotten Naomi and Ruth, nor, by extension, the people of God. Those who so desperately need a king will be provided with one. First there is a summary showing how God filled Naomi's emptiness with satisfaction (4:13-17), and then there is a genealogy pointing to God's ongoing work through this family (v 18-21). It is tempting to read past genealogies without pondering their significance, but this genealogy is vital to understanding what is taking place in *Ruth*: a bigger story is being told.

The narrator shows us four ways God was at work in the lives of Naomi, Ruth, and Boaz, accomplishing his far-reaching purposes through them: God provides a son for Boaz and Ruth, a redeemer for Naomi, a king for Israel, and the Messiah for the world.

"So Boaz took Ruth, and she became his wife. And he went in to her, and the LORD gave her conception, and she bore a son" (v 13). From wedding to baby in one verse!

The Lord's involvement in the birth of this child is not just an important statement for the love story of Boaz and Ruth; it is also part of an important thread in the grand story of the Bible. Throughout the biblical narrative, God intervenes in order to bring forth children who are significant in redemptive history. In each case, God is saying, *Keep your eye on this child! He will play a vital role in accomplishing my purposes.*

In Moab, during ten years of marriage, Ruth did not have children, but now the Lord enables her to have a son. We are left to wonder, "What role will this child play in the advancement of God's purposes?"

Naomi once said that "the hand of the LORD has gone out against me" (1:13), but in fact God's hand was with Naomi. He gave her a child.

Naomi's journey from emptiness to fullness is illustrated in the next sentence: "Then Naomi took the child and laid him on her lap and became his nurse" (v 16). She was empty, having no food and no child. Now, her arms are full—holding this little boy.

God had not forgotten Naomi. She had gone from emptiness to fullness, from bitterness to happiness.

The book of *Ruth* is not just a story about two desperate widows—it is a story about a desperate nation. Remember the last verse in Judges: "There was no king in Israel" (Judges 21:25). It was a broken nation whose immorality and disunity threatened its survival (Judges 21:16-18). Remember the first person mentioned in *Ruth*: Elimelech, "My God is King" (Ruth 1:2). But Elimelech did not live up to his name, and he certainly did not lead Israel out of darkness—far from it. He fled to Moab and died. Obed, however, his grandson by levirate marriage, would be the grandfather of David, the king who would solve Israel's problem by giving God's people leadership, unity, and security. And Obed would also be the ancestor of the King who would solve the world's problem by bringing perfect leadership and complete forgiveness and eternal life.

OPTIONAL EXTRA

In this study, you'll be referring to the genealogy in Matthew 1:1-17. So how about reading it aloud, but swapping the person reading it every time a name changes? For example:

Voice 1: "This is the genealogy of Jesus the Messiah the son of"

Voice 2: "David, the son of"

Voice 3: "Abraham…"

As well as being fun, this will highlight some of the names in Jesus' family tree.

GUIDANCE FOR QUESTIONS

1. Do you know any children who show a strong family likeness with one of their parents? It could be a visual likeness, a similar character trait, the same laugh or smile… In this study we'll see how Obed was going to have a character similar to his mother, Ruth—and how, as Christians, we grow in family likeness with God, our Father, and Jesus, our Brother.

2. In Study 1 (page 7) we created Ruth's family tree. Now use verses 21-22 to fill in the next few generations. If you're not sure of the final name, check Matthew 1:17.

See family tree at bottom of page.

3. In Ruth 4:13-22 we see that God provides a son for Boaz and Ruth, a

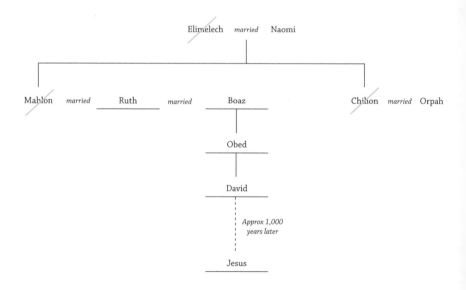

Elimelech *married* Naomi

Mahlon *married* Ruth *married* Boaz   Chilion *married* Orpah

Obed

David

Approx 1,000 years later

Jesus

redeemer for Naomi, a king for Israel, and the Messiah for the world. Which verse matches each of these four gifts from God?

• **A son for Boaz and Ruth:** Ruth 4:13

• **A redeemer for Naomi:** Ruth 4:14

• **A king for Israel:** Ruth 4:17 and 22

• **The Messiah for the world (see also Matthew 1:1):** Ruth 4:17 and 22

4. How has Ruth's status changed from Ruth 1 to Ruth 4? See Ruth 1:4-5, 22; 2:10, 13; 3:9; 4:13. It is encouraging to look back at Ruth's story and see how far she has come. She has been repeatedly called "the Moabite." She called herself the "foreigner" (2:10). She identified herself as being lower than a servant (2:13). She then elevated herself to the level of "servant" when proposing to Boaz (3:9). But here in chapter 4, she is Ruth, the wife of Boaz (4:13). She has a brand new status, thanks to the sovereign grace of God. Not only this, but he gives her a child.

EXPLORE MORE
Throughout the biblical narrative, God intervenes in order to bring forth children who are significant in redemptive history. Often these children are born of women who were previously childless—something which highlights the fact that it is the Lord who provides these births. Investigate one or more of their stories.

(Maybe split your group into smaller groups to look at one or two of these women each.)

• In Genesis 21, Sarah cannot conceive until the Lord intervenes (Genesis 21:1). As a result, Isaac is born even when she is past the menopause (18:10-15; 21:2-3).

• In Genesis 25, Isaac's wife Rebecca is also unable to have children, but the Lord answers Isaac's prayer and she conceives, giving birth to Jacob and Esau (25:21-26).

• In Genesis 29 – 30, God enables both Leah and barren Rachel, the mothers of the people of God, to conceive.

• Later in the Bible, Hannah is barren, but the Lord grants her the ability to have a son: Samuel, who will herald the coming of King David (1 Samuel 1:19-20).

In each case, God is saying, *Keep your eye on this child! He will play a vital role in accomplishing my purposes.*

• **How is Ruth's story similar to theirs?** In *Ruth*, the narrator wants us to know that Ruth belongs to this significant group of mothers, just as the women at the city gate prayed (Ruth 4:11). In Moab, during ten years of marriage, she did not have children, but now the Lord enables her to have a son. Ruth carries her child to full term until "she bore a son." We are left to wonder, "What role will this child play in the advancement of God's purposes?"

5. In Ruth 1, we saw how Naomi changed her name. What did she change it to and why (Ruth 1:20-21)? "Naomi" means "pleasant." She changed her name to "Mara" which means "bitter". She said that "the Almighty has made my life very bitter" (v 20, NIV). "I went away full" (with a husband and two sons) "but the LORD has brought me back empty" (v 21) after her husband and sons all died.

• **How have things changed for Naomi by Ruth 4:14-17?** Naomi has gone from emptiness to fullness. The women around Naomi recognize this transformation. When Naomi first entered town, the ladies asked, "Is this Naomi?" Naomi responded to the buzz in town by insisting that she be called "Mara" ("bitter") instead of

Naomi ("sweet"). But now, a great reversal has taken place. The women of Bethlehem recognize this: their congratulations for the birth of the child go not to Ruth, but to Naomi.

- **What did the women say Ruth's child would do for Naomi (v 15)? Why do you think they were confident of this?** The women's expressed confidence is related to Ruth. How can we be sure that this child will restore and nourish Naomi? The women point to his mother. They are guaranteeing the child's future care of Naomi on the basis of Ruth's character— on Ruth's love for Naomi. Ruth's devotion to Naomi is so great that having her is better than having seven sons. Seven was a number of perfection and sons were highly prized. This expression is the ultimate tribute to Ruth's amazing life and loyalty. The child will be concerned for the wellbeing of Naomi. This is because of God's *hesed*, his kindness, worked through the *hesed* of Ruth, who has displayed remarkable devotion to Naomi from the beginning to the end of this narrative.

6. APPLY: The women were confident that Obed would have a similar character to his mother, Ruth. Christians have God as our loving Father and Jesus as our rescuing Brother. How have you seen your own character changing to show more of a family likeness with your Father and Brother? Sometimes, other people see changes in our lives more easily than we do, so if some of your group are struggling with this question, ask the others if there are positive character changes that they have noticed.

7. What was the historical background to the book of *Ruth*? Ruth is set "in the days when the judges ruled" (Ruth 1:1). At that time, the nation of Israel had no king to lead them in God's ways (Judges 21:25). Instead, everyone simply did what they thought was right.

- **Why does this make the last few verses of Ruth 4 so important?** The book of *Ruth* is not just a story about two desperate widows—it is a story about a desperate nation. It was a broken nation whose immorality and disunity threatened its survival (Judges 21:16-18). Remember the first person mentioned in *Ruth*: Elimelech, "My God is King" (Ruth 1:2). But Elimelech did not live up to his name, and he certainly did not lead Israel out of darkness—far from it. He fled to Moab and died. Obed, however, his grandson by levirate marriage, would be the grandfather of David, the king who would solve Israel's problem by giving God's people leadership, unity, and security. And Obed would also be the ancestor of the King who would solve the world's problem by bringing perfect leadership and complete forgiveness and eternal life.

8. Read Matthew 1:1-6a. How are verses 3b-6a similar to Ruth 4:18-22? Matthew 1:1-17 is the genealogy (line of descent, family tree) of Jesus. Matthew 1:3b-6a lists the same ten people, in the same order, as Ruth 4:18-22.

- **Women were not usually included in genealogies, since descent was traced through the men. Which women have been included in Jesus' genealogy? (See also Matthew 1:3a, 6b, 16.)** Five women have been included: Tamar (v 3), Rahab (v 5), Ruth (v 5), Bathsheba, called "the wife of Uriah" (v 6), and Mary (v 16).

- **These women included a prostitute, a Moabite, and an adulterer. Why is it surprising that these women are** in Jesus' family tree? What does it teach us about the people God uses to work his purposes out? We might think that God's perfect Messiah-King would come from a perfect family line, but these women were far from perfect. They include someone who slept with her father-in-law (Tamar), a prostitute (Rahab), a Moabite (Ruth), an adulterer (Bathsheba), and an unmarried mother (Mary). The genealogy in Matthew 1 makes it clear that God has always saved broken sinners, incorporated them into his people, and used them to further his plans. This genealogy includes prostitutes, adulterers, liars, and murderers. It includes both men and women, both Jews and non-Jews. None are disqualified from being used by God. Here they are in the genealogy of Jesus, his Son, our Messiah!

⩔

- If you have time, read about some of these women:
  - Tamar (Genesis 38)
  - Rahab (Joshua 2:1-21; 6:25)
  - Bathsheba (2 Samuel 11)
  - Mary (Matthew 1:18-25)

These notes will help if you want to discuss any of these women further.

The first lady Matthew lists is Tamar (v 3), the mother of Perez and Zerah, who had deceived and slept with her own father-in-law, Judah (Genesis 38). Then Matthew mentions Rahab (Matthew 1:5). She was a prostitute in Jericho who saved two Israelite spies and became part of God's people (Joshua 2:1-21; 6:25); most notably for our study of *Ruth*, she was the mother of Boaz. Third, Matthew notes Ruth herself, the Moabite.

In the second set of 14 names, in which Israel's kings up to the exile are listed (Matthew 1:6-11), Matthew mentions

Bathsheba, calling her "the wife of Uriah" (v 6). This reminds us that Bathsheba, the mother of King Solomon, was brought into the family line through adultery and murder (2 Samuel 11). Finally, the concluding set of 14 generations goes from the deportation to Babylon to the birth of Jesus Christ (Matthew 1:12-16). There we find the fifth woman to be mentioned: Mary (v 16).

It is unexpected enough to mention women in a genealogy of this time, but when we consider the stories of these particular women, we may be even more surprised. This genealogy demonstrates the fact that God redeems and works his purposes out through sinners. Judah and David were both mighty and significant men, but it is their extramarital unions with Tamar and Bathsheba that are mentioned, and this serves to highlight their sin.

The stories of both Rahab and Ruth, meanwhile, show us how the unlikeliest outsiders—a prostitute in Jericho and a widow from Moab—can end up playing a significant role in the plans of God.

As we read the story of the inclusion of Ruth into the family of Boaz—which is also the family of Judah, Tamar, Perez, and Rahab—and hear the genealogy of her descendants leading up to David, we should remember that she is only one example of a pattern that runs throughout the history of God's people, and that culminates with Jesus: the saving of sinners.

9. In Ruth 4:14-15 we read that Obed was going to be a "redeemer," "a restorer of life and a nourisher of ... old age." Matthew 1 tells us how an even more significant son was born in Bethlehem. How was Jesus even better

than Obed? (See Matthew 1:21-23.)
Obed was "a redeemer" (Ruth 4:14), but
Jesus Christ is our Redeemer, who came
into the world to "save his people from their
sins" (Matthew 1:21).

Matthew 1:23 tells us that Jesus will be
called "Immanuel," which means "God with
us." Not only has God not forgotten us, but
God is *with us*. By placing our faith in Jesus
Christ, we find ultimate refuge, ultimate
rest, and ultimate peace. He has come to
give rest to the weak and weary, the sick
and sore.

**10. APPLY: Think back over the book of
Ruth. How has it pointed you to Jesus?
What have you been most helped by?
What challenge will you take away with
you?** Answers will vary. Encourage everyone
to give at least one thing that has either
helped or challenged them.

Good Book Guides
The full range

2 Corinthians:
7 Studies
Gary Millar
ISBN: 9781784983895

Galatians: 7 Studies
Timothy Keller
ISBN: 9781908762566

Ephesians: 10 Studies
Thabiti Anyabwile
ISBN: 9781907377099

Ephesians: 8 Studies
Richard Coekin
ISBN: 9781910307694

Philippians: 7 Studies
Steven J. Lawson
ISBN: 9781784981181

Colossians: 6 Studies
Mark Meynell
ISBN: 9781906334246

1 Thessalonians:
7 Studies
Mark Wallace
ISBN: 9781904889533

1&2 Timothy: 7 Studies
Phillip Jensen
ISBN: 9781784980191

Titus: 5 Studies
Tim Chester
ISBN: 9781909919631

Hebrews: 8 Studies
Justin Buzzard
ISBN: 9781906334420

James: 6 Studies
Sam Allberry
ISBN: 9781910307816

1 Peter: 6 Studies
Juan R. Sanchez
ISBN: 9781784980177

1 John: 7 Studies
Nathan Buttery
ISBN: 9781904889953

Revelation: 7 Studies
Tim Chester
ISBN: 9781910307021

TOPICAL

Man of God: 10 Studies
Anthony Bewes & Sam
Allberry
ISBN: 9781904889977

Biblical Womanhood:
10 Studies
Sarah Collins
ISBN: 9781907377532

The Apostles' Creed:
10 Studies
Tim Chester
ISBN: 9781905564415

**Promises Kept: Bible
Overview:** 9 Studies
Carl Laferton
ISBN: 9781908317933

The Reformation Solas
6 Studies
Jason Helopoulos
ISBN: 9781784981501

Contentment: 6 Studies
Anne Woodcock
ISBN: 9781905564668

Women of Faith:
8 Studies
Mary Davis
ISBN: 9781904889526

Meeting Jesus: 8 Studies
Jenna Kavonic
ISBN: 9781905564460

Heaven: 6 Studies
Andy Telfer
ISBN: 9781909919457

Making Work Work:
8 Studies
Marcus Nodder
ISBN: 9781908762894

The Holy Spirit: 8 Studies
Pete & Anne Woodcock
ISBN: 9781905564217

Experiencing God:
6 Studies
Tim Chester
ISBN: 9781906334437

Real Prayer: 7 Studies
Anne Woodcock
ISBN: 9781910307595

Mission: 7 Studies
Alan Purser
ISBN: 9781784983628

Dive deeper into the book of Ruth

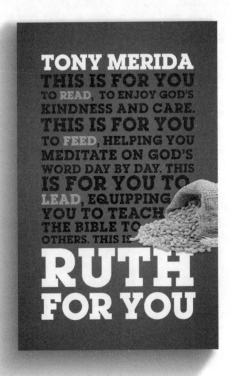

The book of Ruth is a love story. Like all love stories it has twists and turns, tension and resolution, and a happy ending. But it's far more than that because it reveals to us a God who is deeply committed to caring for his people. In Boaz, God provides Ruth with a loving husband to free and provide for her, pointing us to the Bible's grand story of redemption and David's greatest son, Jesus. Tony Merida's compelling story-telling and Christ-centered insights make this an accessible and absorbing expository guide to the book of Ruth. It can be used for personal devotions, or for leading small-group studies, or for sermon preparation.

God's Word For You

Galatians For You

"The book of Galatians is dynamite. It is an explosion of joy and freedom which leaves us enjoying a life of blessing. I pray that it explodes in your heart as you read this book."

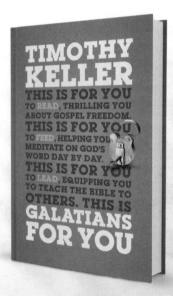
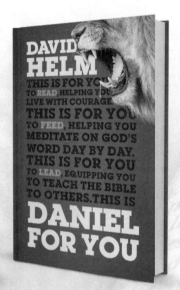

Daniel For You

"The book of Daniel offers you the knowledge that God is still at work, the confidence that it is possible to remain faithful to Jesus Christ, and the strength to live for him in our day."

The Whole Series

Find out more about these resources at:

www.thegoodbook.com/for-you

Join the *explore* community

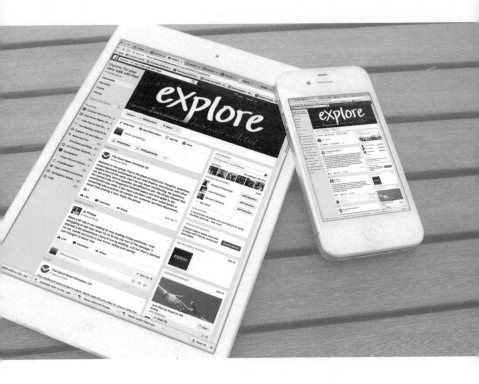

The *Explore* Facebook group is a community of people who use *Explore* to study the Bible each day.

This is the place to share your thoughts, questions, encouragements, and prayers as you read *Explore*, and interact with other readers, as well as contributors, from around the world. No questions are too simple or too difficult to ask.

JOIN NOW:
facebook.com/groups/tgbc.explore

thegoodbook
COMPANY

BIBLICAL | RELEVANT | ACCESSIBLE

At The Good Book Company, we are dedicated to helping Christians and local churches grow. We believe that God's growth process always starts with hearing clearly what he has said to us through his timeless word—the Bible.

Ever since we opened our doors in 1991, we have been striving to produce Bible-based resources that bring glory to God. We have grown to become an international provider of user-friendly resources to the Christian community, with believers of all backgrounds and denominations using our books, Bible studies, devotionals, evangelistic resources, and DVD-based courses.

We want to equip ordinary Christians to live for Christ day by day, and churches to grow in their knowledge of God, their love for one another, and the effectiveness of their outreach.

Call us for a discussion of your needs or visit one of our local websites for more information on the resources and services we provide.

Your friends at The Good Book Company

thegoodbook.com | thegoodbook.co.uk
thegoodbook.com.au | thegoodbook.co.nz
thegoodbook.co.in